INTRODUCTION TO ADA

David Price

Prentice-Hall, Inc.
Englewood Cliffs, N.J. 07632

Library of Congress Cataloging in Publication Data

Price, David, 1961–
Introduction to Ada.

Includes index.
1. Ada (Computer program language) I. Title.
QA76.73.A35P74 1984 001.64'24 83-16082
ISBN 0-13-477653-4
ISBN 0-13-477646-1 (pbk.)

Editorial/production supervision and
interior design: *Aliza Greenblatt*

Cover design: *Jeannette Jacobs*

Manufacturing buyer: *Gordon Osbourne*

Printed in the United States of America

10 9 8 7 6 5 4 3 2 1

ISBN 0-13-477646-1 {P}
ISBN 0-13-477653-4 {C}

PRENTICE-HALL INTERNATIONAL, INC., *London*
PRENTICE-HALL OF AUSTRALIA PTY. LIMITED, *Sydney*
EDITORA PRENTICE-HALL DO BRASIL, LTDA., *Rio de Janeiro*
PRENTICE-HALL CANADA INC., *Toronto*
PRENTICE-HALL OF INDIA PRIVATE LIMITED, *New Delhi*
PRENTICE-HALL OF JAPAN, INC., *Tokyo*
PRENTICE-HALL OF SOUTHEAST ASIA PTE. LTD., *Singapore*
WHITEHALL BOOKS LIMITED, *Wellington, New Zealand*

CONTENTS

PREFACE vii

1 Fundamentals 1

1.1 Some short programs in Ada *1* ***1.2 Integer expressions*** *4* ***1.3 Object declarations*** *7* ***1.4 Input and output*** *9*

2 Conditional Execution 12

2.1 Boolean expressions *12* ***2.2 Branching*** *16* ***2.3 Looping*** *20* ***2.4 Counted looping*** *23* ***2.5 Exceptional transfer*** *25*

3 Type Declarations 27

3.1 Enumeration types *27* ***3.2 Subtypes*** *30* ***3.3 Derived types*** *32* ***3.4 Type attributes*** *34*

4 Other Numeric Types 37

4.1 Floating point types *37* ***4.2 Fixed point types*** *39* ***4.3 Based numbers*** *41* ***4.4 Formatting numeric output*** *42*

5 **Arrays** **44**
5.1 Constrained array declarations 44
5.2 Unconstrained array declarations 48
5.3 Aggregates and slices 50 5.4 String variables 54

6 **Records** **61**
6.1 Invariant records 61 6.2 Size-variant records 64 6.3 Type-variant records 67

7 **Subprograms** **70**
7.1 Function subprograms 70 7.2 Procedure subprograms 73 7.3 Scope and visibility 76
7.4 Subprogram overloading 78

8 **Access Types** **82**
8.1 Scalar type allocation 82 8.2 Composite type allocation 84 8.3 Stacks 87 8.4 Lists and trees 90

9 **Packages** **96**
9.1 Package declarations 96 9.2 Private types and deferred constants 99 9.3 Limited private types 102 9.4 Library packages 103
9.5 Benefits of isolation 105

10 **Exceptions** **108**
10.1 Predefined exceptions 108 10.2 Handling an exception 109 10.3 Raising an exception 111
10.4 Exceptions and robustness 113

11 **Generic Declarations** **115**
11.1 Instantiation and formal types 115
11.2 Type matching 118 11.3 Subprogram matching 121

12 **Files** **124**
12.1 Text file formatting *124* ***12.2 File management*** *126* ***12.3 Sequential file operations*** *129* ***12.4 Direct file operations*** *131*

A **Appendix: Reserved Words** **134**

B **Appendix: ASCII Character Set** **135**

C **Appendix: Library Package STANDARD** **138**

D **Appendix: Library Package TEXT_IO** **143**

Index **149**

PREFACE

This book is meant to serve as an introduction to the programming language Ada. The reader is not presumed to have extensive programming experience or advanced mathematical training. Only one prerequisite is essential: an interest in the Ada language. The aim of this book is to guide the reader through Ada programming concepts with a minimum of confusion or intimidation.

Though the development of Ada was sponsored by the U.S. Department of Defense, Ada is not limited to a handful of specific applications. It is, in fact, a powerful general-purpose tool. In many ways, it is a proper superset of other popular languages. At the time of its introduction, the uses projected for it ranged from controlling small computers embedded in machinery to maintaining the records of large businesses. A working knowledge of Ada, then, is likely to be an important stock-in-trade among professional programmers for many years to come.

Some aspects of the language may appear to be idiosyncratic or even cumbersome at first glance. They will be especially evident in the early chapters of this book, where most of the example programs will be quite small. The reason behind them lies in the fact that Ada is designed to simplify the production of large programs. Since the complexity of a program increases rapidly as the program becomes larger, Ada provides a number of facilities for dividing programs into smaller modules. These facilities help make Ada programs easier to read, to write, and to modify.

At this writing, most books about Ada are based on outdated descriptions of the language. This book, however, was written to be consistent with the draft Ada standard released in July 1982. Though minor editorial changes may follow in later standards, substantial revisions to this definition of the language are unlikely. Hence, the descriptions of Ada's features in this book are not in danger of becoming obsolete.

I am grateful to Charles Wetherall of Bell Laboratories for many insightful comments. (The remaining defects of the book are, of course, my responsibility.)

I am also grateful to James F. Fegen, Jr. and his associates at Prentice-Hall for their support of this project. Finally, I am grateful to my family and friends for their sympathetic patience.

DAVID PRICE
Midlothian, Virginia

1

FUNDAMENTALS

1.1 SOME SHORT PROGRAMS IN ADA

Suppose we wanted to write a program in Ada for multiplying a pair of numbers. What would the completed program look like? This is obviously not the sort of problem to which a programmer would devote a great deal of attention in practice, but it will suit our purposes here quite well. In this section we will examine three programs for multiplying numbers; we will use these programs to become acquainted with the style and structure of the Ada language.

Example 1.1

```
with TEXT_IO; use TEXT_IO;
procedure FIRST_MULTIPLY is
    I,J : INTEGER;
    package INT_IO is new INTEGER_IO(INTEGER);
    use INT_IO;
begin
    I := 17;
    J := 60;
    PUT(I*J);
end FIRST_MULTIPLY;
```

The program shown in example 1.1 prints the product of 17 and 60. The lines started by the words *with, package,* and *use* are included for "housekeeping" purposes; we will return to them in section 1.4. Aside from housekeeping, the program has three parts: the *header,* the *declarations,* and the *body*. The header simply indicates the program name. (This program has been given the name FIRST_MULTIPLY.) The declarations list the programmer-defined entities that will be used inside the program. In this program, the names I and J are declared to represent integer variables. Finally, the body of the program lists the instructions that the computer will follow in executing the program.

In the header line, the name of the program is enclosed by the words *procedure* and *is*. These words are called *reserved words* in Ada because they are reserved for a particular purpose. The word *procedure,* for instance, indicates that we are reading the header line. Other reserved words are set aside for other situations. Although no typographical distinction is needed in an actual program, reserved words appear in lower case throughout this book to make the sample programs more readable.

Each variable in an Ada program is associated with a *data type*. The data type of a variable indicates, as you would expect, the type of data that the variable can hold. In this program, I and J are declared to have the type INTEGER. A variable of type INTEGER can store one integer number. In later chapters we will use data types that can represent other forms of data, such as rational numbers or matrices. Until then, our sample programs will use variables of type INTEGER.

Like the program name, the program body is surrounded by a pair of reserved words. The reserved word *begin* precedes the body; the reserved word *end* follows it. The first two lines of the program shown in example 1.1 assign values to the variables I and J. Statements in this form are called *assignment* statements. The two-character symbol ':=' is called the *assignment operator*.

The final statement in the body of this program is a PUT statement. PUT is a predefined "subprogram" that accepts a value and prints it. In this case, PUT has been given the expression I*J. When the PUT statement is reached, this expression will be evaluated; the current values of the variables will be substituted where they appear. Since I and J will equal 17 and 60 when the PUT is reached, the value of I*J will be 17*60, or 1020. Hence, the value 1020 will be printed.

Example 1.2

```
with TEXT_IO; use TEXT_IO;
program SECOND_MULTIPLY is
    I,J,PRODUCT : INTEGER;
    package INT_IO is new INTEGER_IO(INTEGER);
    use INT_IO;
begin
    I:= 17;
    J:= 60;
    PRODUCT:= I * J;
    PUT(PRODUCT);
end SECOND_MULTIPLY;
```

The program shown in example 1.2 illustrates the use of expressions in assignment statements. When the third assignment is encountered, PRODUCT will be assigned the value of the expression. Any valid expression can appear in the right-hand part of an assignment statement, as long as both sides of the assignment have the same data type. For instance, if the variable on the left of the assignment operator is of type INTEGER, then the expression on the right should yield a value of type INTEGER. (We discuss the other arithmetic operations available for use with integers in the following section.)

The names that can be chosen for variables are subject to some constraints. Program names are subject to these constraints as well. In fact, variable names and program names fall into the same lexical category: both are examples of *identifiers*. Here are the rules governing identifiers:

1. The first character of an identifier must be a letter.
2. Subsequent characters of an identifier may include letters, digits, and underscores.
3. An identifier can have any number of characters.
4. A programmer-declared identifier cannot conflict with a reserved word. (Appendix A gives a list of Ada's reserved words.)

Here are some valid identifiers:

```
MY_NAME
Number
X
Count3
NEXT_LINE_OF_TEXT
```

Here are some invalid identifiers:

```
16BASE          --begins with a digit
Name&Age        --contains an invalid symbol
```

Notice that the fourth rule disallows variable names like BEGIN or END, which are already reserved by Ada. Importantly, differences in upper case and lower case letters do not make identifiers distinct from one another. Hence, the identifiers PAGE, Page, and pAGe are treated as if they referred to the same entity. All other distinctions are significant, however. The identifiers BIRTH_DAY and BIRTHDAY, for instance, are distinct because one has an underscore and the other does not.

Example 1.3

```
with TEXT_IO; use TEXT_IO;
procedure THIRD_MULTIPLY is
    I,J,PRODUCT : INTEGER ;
    package INT_IO is new INTEGER_IO(INTEGER) ;
    use TEXT_IO, INT_IO ;
begin
    GET(I) ;      --read the first number
    GET(J) ;      --read the second number
    PRODUCT := I * J ;      --multiply them
    PUT(PRODUCT) ;      --print the result
end THIRD_MULTIPLY ;
```

The program shown in example 1.3 introduces two additional features of the language. First, the statements in the body are annotated with *comments*. A comment has no effect on program execution; its purpose is to make the program easier for a human reader to understand. To place a comment in an Ada program, we simply precede it with a pair of hyphens. A comment can be placed on the same line as a program statement or on a separate line altogether. Since the characters following the hyphens are ignored, a comment cannot be followed by another statement on the same line. For instance, the assignment that appears in the comment below will not be executed:

```
--now we will add.  X := 5 + 3;
```

The second feature introduced in example 1.3 is the GET statement. Like PUT, GET is a predefined subprogram that can be invoked within another program. It accepts a value from the user and places the value in the specified variable. In example 1.3 it is used to fetch values for I and J.

The use of GET obviously makes THIRD_MULTIPLY far more flexible than SECOND_MULTIPLY. The latter can calculate the product of only one pair of numbers, while the former allows the user to enter a new pair each time the program is run. We will return to the subject of input and output in section 1.4 and again in later chapters.

Before going further, we should note the use of semicolons as punctuation in Ada programs. The semicolon is used in Ada to terminate statements. Regrettably, this rule is easier to state than to use in practice, because no comparable rule is available to define what a "statement" is in loose terms. The program header is not regarded as a separate statement, for instance, while the entries in the variable declarations are. The best route to familiarity with Ada's semicolon rules is simply to follow the usage shown in the sample programs.

1.2 INTEGER EXPRESSIONS

Ada provides ten arithmetic operators for use with integers. Three of the operators are *unary* operators; that is, they accept a single value and return a single value. The others are *binary* operators, meaning that they accept a pair of values. The unary operators are

+	for identity
−	for negation
abs	for absolute value

The binary operators are

+	for addition
−	for subtraction
*	for multiplication
/	for division
mod	for modulus

rem for remainder
** for exponentiation

The unary operators, along with the first three binary operators, are equivalent to their counterparts in conventional arithmetic. Here are some expressions written with these operators:

```
X * X            --square of X
-SIGN            --negative of SIGN
+I               --same as I
4 + 6            --10
abs (4 - 6)      --2
```

When used with integers, the division operator differs from conventional division. This difference arises because an arithmetic operator in Ada always returns a value that has the same type as its operands. For operations like addition and multiplication, this is consistent with conventional arithmetic: the sum of two integers is always an integer, for instance, as is the product of two integers. With division, however, the rule creates a discrepancy, because integer division in Ada returns only the integer part of the quotient. Thus, the integer expression 5/2 yields 2, not 2.5.

The operators *mod* and *rem* are provided so that programmers can circumvent this discrepancy. These operators return the remainder from a division operation. Given a pair of positive integers *i* and *j*, we can find the remainder of i/j with either of the following expressions:

```
i rem j
i mod j
```

For positive integers, the following identity holds:

```
i mod j = i rem j = i - (i/j)*j
```

If the two integers have different signs, then the two operators have slightly different effects. When one operand is positive and the other is negative, the identity above does not hold for *mod*. The following identity holds instead:

```
i mod j = i - (i/j)*j + j
```

Here are some expressions in which these operators appear:

```
7/3              --equals 2
7 rem 3          --equals 1
7 mod 3          --equals 1
-7/-3            --equals 2
-7 rem -3        --equals 1
-7 mod -3        --equals 1
-7/3             --equals -2
-7 rem 3         --equals -1
```

```
-7 mod 3      --equals 2
7/-3          --equals -2
7 rem -3      --equals 1
7 mod -3      --equals -2
```

When used with integers, the exponentiation operator requires that the right operand (i.e., the exponent) be a nonnegative value. If the exponent is zero, then the operation returns the value 1, as with ordinary exponent operations. Here are some examples of expressions in which the exponentiation operator is used:

```
X ** 2      --square of X
J ** 0      --equals 1 for any J
2 ** BITS
M ** N
A*(X**2) + B*X + C
```

Expressions in Ada are evaluated according to rules of operator precedence similar to the standard precedence rules of algebra. Each operator has a level of precedence that determines the order in which the components of an expression will be processed. Four levels of precedence are defined for the integer operators:

```
**
* / mod rem
+ - abs      --unary
+ -          --binary
```

When an integer expression is encountered, the exponentiation operations are performed first; binary additions and subtractions are performed last. When an expression contains several operators on the same level of precedence, they are evaluated from left to right. Thus,

```
10 + 6 * 2      --equals 22, not 32
2 ** 3 + 1      --equals 9, not 16
10*3/2          --equals 15, not 10
```

Parentheses can be inserted in an expression to override the precedence rules. Thus,

```
(10 + 6) * 2      --equals 32
2**(3 + 1)        --equals 16
10 * (3/2)        --equals 10
```

When writing large integers, we can use two options provided by Ada to make them more readable. First, we can insert underscores in them to separate groups of digits. These embedded underscores have no effect on the value of the number. Hence, the following integers all have the same value:

```
1234567
123_4567
1_234_567
```

Second, we can use scientific notation. A number written in scientific notation has two parts: a *mantissa* and an *exponent*. In the form of scientific notation provided by Ada, the mantissa and the exponent are separated by an *E* or an *e*. A number written in scientific notation is equal to the mantissa multiplied by ten to the power of the exponent. For example:

```
5e0     --equals 5
5E1     --equals 50
5E2     --equals 500
0e2     --equals 0
```

An integer written in scientific notation cannot have a negative exponent. Ada imposes this restriction because raising a number to a negative power generally yields a noninteger result. Of course, no such restriction applies to the mantissa.

1.3 OBJECT DECLARATIONS

In Ada, the term *object* refers to a place where values can be stored. A variable is one kind of object; other kinds of objects include *constants* and *numbers*. This section will examine declarations for all three. We have seen some examples of variable declarations already. In general, a variable declaration takes the form of a list of identifiers followed by the name of the desired type. Variable declarations may also specify the value that the variables will initially have. Here are some examples of variable declarations:

```
SUM : INTEGER ;
P , Q : INTEGER ;
SALES1 , SALES2 , SALES3 : INTEGER := 0 ;
```

The first declaration creates an integer variable named SUM. The second creates integer variables named P and Q. The third creates integer variables named SALES1, SALES2, and SALES3 and assigns them an initial value of 0. The practice of initializing a variable within its declaration offers several advantages. First, it eliminates the need to write an additional assignment in the body of the program. Second, it makes the initial value of the variable easier for a human reader to find. Third, and most usefully, it prevents "undefined value" errors—i.e., it eliminates the possibility that the program will attempt to access the variable before it has been given a value.

The initial value specified in a variable declaration can be an expression. If the expression includes other variables, then those variables must be declared and initialized first. Here is a sequence of declarations in which this requirement is met:

```
MASS : INTEGER := 10 ;
ACCEL : INTEGER := 5 ;
FORCE : INTEGER := MASS * ACCEL ;
```

In this case, FORCE will be initialized to 50. Transposing the declarations for FORCE and ACCEL, however, would make the sequence invalid. Here is another sequence of declarations that meets the requirement:

```
POS1 : INTEGER := -3;
POS2 : INTEGER := 7;
LENGTH : INTEGER := abs (POS1 - POS2);
```

A constant declaration associates an identifier with a value that remains unchanged during program execution. Constant declarations have the same form as variable declarations, except that the type identifier is preceded by the reserved word *constant*. Here are some examples of constant declarations:

```
Freezing__Point : constant INTEGER := 0;
SPEED__LIMIT : constant INTEGER := 55;
CAPACITY : constant INTEGER := 2e5;
LOAD : constant INTEGER := CAPACITY/3;
```

As with variable declarations, the value specified in a constant declaration may be an expression. Variables and constants can appear interchangeably in constant and variable declarations, as long as the declarations are made in a valid order. Unlike a variable, however, a constant cannot be assigned a new value in the body of the program.

A number declaration is similar to a constant declaration, with two differences. First, a number declaration does not include a type identifier; the type of the value is determined by inspection. Second, the value specified in a number declaration must be given as a *static expression*. A static expression is one that can be evaluated before the program runs. The only values that can appear in a static numeric expression are literals, constants declared with static expressions, and declared number identifiers. A literal is an explicit value, like "– 10" or "3e4." The only operations that can be performed in a static expression are the predefined operations, such as addition and multiplication. Here are some examples of valid number declarations:

```
DOUBLE__BYTE : constant := 2 ** 16;
Line__Size : constant := 80;
Lines : constant := 24;
Page__Size : constant := Line__Size*Lines;
```

Constant and number declarations are useful when a certain value is likely to be used many times throughout a program. First, associating such a value with a symbolic identifier makes the program easier to understand. When we read a program for the first time, we will doubtless find it more comprehensible if the programmer used identifiers instead of unexplained literals. Second, constant and number declarations make a program easier to transport and modify. If we want to alter a machine-dependent value, say, we can do so more quickly and reliably if the value has been associated with an identifier. It is obviously far simpler to modify one line—a constant declaration—than to update every occurrence of the value in the program body.

In Ada parlance, the action of associating an identifier with an entity in the program is called *elaboration*. Just as statements are *executed* and expressions are *evaluated,* declarations in an Ada program are said to be *elaborated*. Taken together, the declarations in an Ada program are termed the *declarative part* of the program.

1.4 INPUT AND OUTPUT

The example programs that appeared earlier in this chapter included a number of cryptic statements. One of them preceded the program headers:

```
with TEXT_IO; use TEXT_IO;
```

The others were placed in the declarative part:

```
package INT_IO is new INTEGER_IO(INTEGER);
use INT_IO;
```

These statements are needed so we can perform input and output in the program body. The first one informs Ada that we will be using input–output subprograms like GET and PUT. The second and third are used to "awaken" the subprograms. To be precise, we should call this awakening process *instantiation*. We will not concern ourselves with the details of instantiation until much later. For now, all we need to know is how to make it work.

A separate instantiation is needed for each data type that will be involved in input or output. In the examples, we used only the type INTEGER. Suppose we are also using GET or PUT with an integer type called WXYZ. We would then write this in the declarative part:

```
package INT_IO is new INTEGER_IO(INTEGER);
package WXYZ_IO is new INTEGER_IO(WXYZ);
use INT_IO, WXYZ_IO;
```

The pattern should now be evident. First, we chose an identifier for each instantiation. (Any identifier is suitable.) For the instantiation of INTEGER input–output we used INT_IO. For WXYZ we used WXYZ_IO. We then placed each one in a different *package . . . is* statement as shown. Finally, we listed them in a *use* clause. Ada's input–output subprograms are now available for the given types.

As used here, GET and PUT control whatever device has been designated the *default file*. We will assume that the default file is a keyboard terminal with a screen or a printer of some kind. The following statement, then, will accept a value from the terminal:

```
GET(USER_ID);
```

Ada uses the type of the variable to determine the type of value to accept. If USER__ID is of type INTEGER, then the given value must be an integer. Otherwise, an error condition will result.

This statement will cause the number 55 to appear at the terminal:

```
PUT(55);
```

This statement will cause the expression WAGE*8 to be evaluated and printed:

```
PUT(WAGE*8);
```

We can also use PUT to print *character strings*. A character string can be any sequence of characters. The contents of a character string are not subject to any rules of syntax. To place a character string in a PUT statement, we simply enclose the string with quotation marks. The quotation marks will not be printed. Here are some PUT statements that print character strings:

```
PUT("This is a test.");
PUT("0123456789");
PUT("!@#$%^&*()-+");
PUT("A quotation mark can appear "" in a string.");
```

The last example demonstrates an exceptional case: namely, the use of quotation marks within strings. Since quotation marks are used as delimiters, Ada requires that quotation marks inside strings be written doubly. This requirement prevents ambiguities. Strings with pairs of quotation marks will be printed in their correct, single-quotation form.

A single PUT statement can print only one value. To print more than one value on a line, we use multiple PUT statements in succession. Here is an example of such a sequence:

```
PUT("The product of");
PUT(X);
PUT("times");
PUT(Y);
PUT("is");
PUT(X*Y);
```

If X equals 5 and Y equals 6, the output will look something like this:

```
The product of 5 times 6 is 30
```

To start a new line, we use the predefined subprogram NEW__LINE. Each time NEW__LINE is encountered, the cursor or print head returns to the first column of the next line. A sequence of NEW__LINE statements will leave extra blank lines. Here is a statement sequence that prints two character strings on separate lines:

```
PUT("This is the first line.");
NEW_LINE;
PUT("This is the second.");
```

Without the NEW_LINE, the two strings would be printed on a single line. Instead, they will be printed as below:

```
This is the first line.
This is the second.
```

Ada provides an additional subprogram, PUT_LINE, that combines PUT and NEW_LINE for strings. If we have a string that is to be the last item on its line, we can use PUT_LINE as below:

```
PUT_LINE("This is the first string.");
PUT("This is the second.");
```

The program shown in example 1.4 is a final embellishment of our multiplication program. It illustrates some of the input–output subprograms described in this section. It also gives a simple illustration of *prompting*. While the program in example 1.3 gave the user no explanation of the values it needed, this program asks (or "prompts") the user more congenially.

Example 1.4

```
with TEXT_IO; use TEXT_IO;
procedure LAST_MULTIPLY is
    I,J : INTEGER;
    package INT_IO is new INTEGER_IO(INTEGER);
    use INT_IO;
begin
    PUT_LINE("What are the two numbers you want multiplied?");
    GET(I);
    GET(J);
    PUT("The product is");
    PUT(I * J);
end LAST_MULTIPLY;
```

We have seen only a handful of Ada's input–output subprograms in this section. These subprograms also have variants that allow greater sophistication. Later chapters (particularly chapter 12) discuss them in more detail.

2

CONDITIONAL EXECUTION

2.1 BOOLEAN EXPRESSIONS

Ada provides a number of facilities for modifying the flow of program control based on the outcome of comparisons and logical operations. Some of these facilities use the data type BOOLEAN to determine the course that the flow of control will take. Unlike variables of type INTEGER, which can have a large number of possible values, a variable of type BOOLEAN can have only two. The two values permitted in the data type BOOLEAN are called *TRUE* and *FALSE*. These identifiers are used to name the boolean values because the boolean type is often used to represent the result of a yes/no query, such as "Does X*3 equal Y?" or perhaps "Is J greater than 1?"

Boolean expressions can include a variety of operands and operators. Among the operands, the most obvious are the literals TRUE and FALSE. In addition, boolean expressions can include variables of type BOOLEAN. Here are two assignment statements that assign boolean values to boolean variables:

```
DEVICE_WORKING := TRUE;
FLAG := FALSE;
```

Three classes of boolean operators are available. The most frequently used operators are the *relational* operators. A relational operator takes two operands of the same type and compares them. The result is a value of type BOOLEAN. The relational operators are written as one- and two-character symbols:

=	equal
/=	not equal

>	greater than
<	less than
>=	greater than or equal
<=	less than or equal

Note that the equality operator (=) is distinct from the assignment operator (:=). Here is a boolean expression that compares two integer values, returning TRUE if they are equal and FALSE if they are not:

```
COUNT = MAX - 1
```

Here is an assignment statement that gives ODD the value TRUE if SUM is odd and gives it the value FALSE otherwise:

```
ODD := (SUM rem 2) = 1;
```

The second class of operators available for use in boolean expressions is the *logical* operators. Ada provides seven logical operators; one of them is unary and the rest are binary. A logical operator takes one or two boolean operands and returns a boolean value. The unary operator, *not,* takes one boolean operand and simply returns its logical negation. That is, it returns TRUE if the operand equals FALSE, and FALSE if the operand equals TRUE. Thus,

```
not TRUE          --equals FALSE
not FALSE         --equals TRUE
```

The binary operator *or* returns TRUE if either or both of its operands equal TRUE. Hence, it returns FALSE only if both of its operands equal FALSE. So,

```
TRUE or TRUE          --equals TRUE
FALSE or FALSE        --equals FALSE
TRUE or FALSE         --equals TRUE
FALSE or TRUE         --equals TRUE
```

The *and* operator returns TRUE only if both of its operands equal TRUE. Otherwise, it yields the value FALSE. So,

```
TRUE and TRUE         --equals TRUE
FALSE and FALSE       --equals FALSE
TRUE and FALSE        --equals FALSE
FALSE and TRUE        --equals FALSE
```

The *xor* operator returns TRUE if one of its operands equals TRUE and one of them equals FALSE. (The abbreviation *xor* stands for *exclusive or*.) Thus,

```
TRUE xor TRUE         --equals FALSE
FALSE xor FALSE       --equals FALSE
```

```
TRUE xor FALSE          --equals TRUE
FALSE xor TRUE          --equals TRUE
```

Logical operators like these are useful when we want to make several comparisons at the same time. For instance, suppose we have measurements from a geometric figure stored in four integer variables named SIDE1, SIDE2, ANGLE1, and ANGLE2. If we wanted to determine whether the two sides were equal and whether the two angles were equal, we would write a boolean expression like

```
(SIDE1=SIDE2) and (ANGLE1=ANGLE2)
```

On the other hand, if we were interested in knowing whether *either* pair of values were equal, we would write something like

```
(SIDE1=SIDE2) or (ANGLE1=ANGLE2)
```

The last two logical operators are called *short circuit control forms*. Unlike the other binary logical operators, whose operands may be evaluated in either order, the operands of a short circuit control form are always evaluated from left to right. The operator *and then* is identical to *and,* except that its right operand is not evaluated unless its left operand is found to equal TRUE. This feature is useful when one of the operands that we want to evaluate is dependent, somehow, on the other. Consider these expressions:

```
(BOTTOM > 0) and (TOP/BOTTOM <= 1)
(BOTTOM > 0) and then (TOP/BOTTOM <= 1)
```

The first boolean expression may fail if BOTTOM equals zero. If the right-hand side is evaluated first, then an attempt to divide by zero will occur. The second boolean expression does not share this danger, however, because the right-hand side will not be evaluated if the left-hand side equals FALSE. When BOTTOM equals zero, the second expression will return the value FALSE without continuing.

Similarly, the *or else* operator is identical to *or,* except that its right operand is not evaluated unless its left operand equals FALSE. Hence,

```
FALSE and then FALSE    --left evaluated
TRUE and then TRUE      --both evaluated
FALSE and then TRUE     --left
TRUE and then FALSE     --both
TRUE or else TRUE       --left
FALSE or else FALSE     --both
TRUE or else FALSE      --left
FALSE or else TRUE      --both
```

The third class of boolean operators is the *membership* operators. The two membership operators are called *in* and *not in*. A membership operator is used to determine whether a value lies within a certain range. We specify a range by separating the lower and upper bounds of the range with two periods. (This notation is used often in Ada.) The bounds can be expressions or literals. Here are some boolean expressions written using the membership operators:

```
COUNT in 1..10
TEMPERATURE not in -20..0
(AGE in 6..10) or (AGE in 13..16)
HOUSE_NUMBER in FIRST_NUM..FIRST_NUM + 100
```

In the order of evaluation applied to boolean expressions, the *not* operator has the highest precedence. The comparison operators and the short circuit control forms occupy an intermediate level of precedence, while the remaining logical operators occupy the lowest. An expression that includes both integer and boolean operators will be evaluated in the following sequence:

```
**
* / mod rem
+ - not abs                        --unary
+ -                                --binary
= /= < <= > >= in   not in
and   or   xor   and then   or else
```

Though parentheses can be used to override the levels of precedence defined for integer and boolean operators, they are not generally needed. A handful of anomalies may arise, however, from the fact that *not* has higher precedence than the comparison operators and some of the arithmetic operators. For this reason, the first expression below will yield an error condition, while the second will produce the expected result:

```
HOURS > 40 or not OVERTIME < 10
HOURS > 40 or not (OVERTIME < 10)
```

In the first case, Ada's precedence rules force an attempt to evaluate the subexpression *not OVERTIME;* since OVERTIME is an integer variable, this is obviously nonsensical. In the second case, parentheses are used to ensure that the *not* is evaluated after the comparison. Here is another pair of expressions that Ada interprets in a surprising way:

```
not WAGE + TIPS > MINIMUM
not (WAGE + TIPS > MINIMUM)
```

Since *not* has precedence over addition, the first expression ends with an attempt to evaluate *not WAGE*. The second expression is evaluated normally. Use of parentheses can avert errors of this kind, as well as increasing the clarity of a tortuous logical relation.

2.2 BRANCHING

Our ability to test program conditions with boolean expressions would be of little value unless we could use the outcome of these tests to affect the execution of the program. Statements that modify the flow of the program are called *control structures*. The simplest control structure that Ada provides, the *if . . . then* structure, allows the program to branch between a number of options based on the value of a boolean expression. The basic form of this structure is

```
if boolean then
    statement;
    statement;
    ...
    statement;
end if;
```

When an *if* is encountered, the given boolean expression is evaluated. If the result is TRUE, then the given sequence of statements is executed. Otherwise, the flow of control passes directly to the statement following the *end if*. Here is an *if* structure in this form:

```
if TEMPERATURE < 0 then
    PUT_LINE("The temperature is freezing.");
    DANGER_ZONE := TRUE;
end if;
```

The program shown in example 2.1 accepts the coefficients for a quadratic equation and reports the number of solutions for it. The three coefficients are represented by integer variables named QUAD, LINEAR, and CONST. Since the *if*'s follow one after the other, each of the boolean conditions will be tested, even after one has been found to be TRUE.

Example 2.1

```
with TEXT_IO; use TEXT_IO;
procedure QUADRATIC is
    QUAD, LINEAR, CONST, RADICAL: INTEGER;
    package INT_IO is new INTEGER_IO(INTEGER);
    use INT_IO;
begin
    PUT_LINE("Please enter the three coefficients of the equation.");
    GET(QUAD);
    GET(LINEAR);
    GET(CONST);
    RADICAL := LINEAR ** 2 - 4*QUAD*CONST;
    if RADICAL < 0 then
        PUT_LINE("This equation has no real roots.");
    end if;
    if RADICAL = 0 then
        PUT_LINE("This equation has one real root.");
    end if;
```

```
    if RADICAL > 0 then
        PUT_LINE("This equation has two real roots.");
    end if;
end QUADRATIC;
```

An *if* structure can be extended with an *else* clause to specify the action that will be taken if the boolean expression is false. When an *else* clause is given, two statement sequences are included in the structure. The sequence that precedes the *else* is executed if the boolean expression equals TRUE; otherwise, the sequence that follows the *else* is executed instead. The program then resumes after the *end if* as before. Here is an example of *if . . . then . . . else:*

```
if AMOUNT_DUE > CREDIT_LIMIT then
    PUT_LINE("The limit has been exceeded.");
    PUT_LINE("Further credit cannot be offered.");
    ACCEPT_ORDER := FALSE;
else
    PUT_LINE("The status of this account is");
    PUT_LINE("acceptable. Credit should be");
    PUT_LINE("granted in the amount of");
    PUT(CREDIT_LIMIT - AMOUNT_DUE);
    ACCEPT_ORDER := TRUE;
end if;
```

Since the conditions tested in example 2.1 are mutually exclusive, we can rewrite that program with nested *if*'s. The new program, shown in example 2.2, does not make redundant tests. (When *else* clauses are used with nested *if*'s, each *else* corresponds to the *if* immediately preceding it.)

Example 2.2

```
with TEXT_IO; use TEXT_IO;
procedure QUICK_QUAD is
    QUAD, LINEAR, CONST : INTEGER;
    RADICAL : INTEGER;
    package INT_IO is new INTEGER_IO(INTEGER);
    use INT_IO;
begin
    GET(QUAD);
    GET(LINEAR);
    GET(CONST);
    RADICAL := LINEAR ** 2 - 4*QUAD*CONST;
    if RADICAL < 0 then
        PUT_LINE("This equation has no real roots.");
    else
        if RADICAL = 0 then
            PUT_LINE("This equation has one real root.");
        else
            PUT_LINE("This equation has two real roots.");
        end if;
    end if;
end QUICK_QUAD;
```

A combination of an *else* followed by another *if* can be abbreviated with the clause *elsif*. The conditional statements in our quadratic program could be rewritten this way:

```
if RADICAL < 0 then
    PUT_LINE("...");
elsif RADICAL = 0 then
    PUT_LINE("...");
else
    PUT_LINE("...");
end if;
```

Ada provides another control structure, the *case* structure, that lets us program a branch using nonboolean expressions. The *case* structure accepts an expression and a list of its possible values. In addition, a list of statement sequences is provided; each sequence corresponds to one of the values. Here is the format of a *case* structure:

```
case expression is
    when choices => statements;
    when choices => statements;
    ...
    when choices => statements;
end case;
```

When a *case* is encountered, the given expression is evaluated. Its value is then located in the lists of choices following each *when*. Finally, the statement sequence corresponding to that value is executed. This *case* structure takes an integer in the range 1 . . 12 and reports the "quarter" in which the equivalent month occurs:

```
case MONTHS is
    when 1,2,3, => PUT_LINE("First quarter");
    when 4,5,6 => PUT_LINE("Second quarter");
    when 7,8,9 => PUT_LINE("Third quarter");
    when 10,11,12 => PUT_LINE("Fourth quarter");
end case;
```

Though the effects of a *case* structure can be duplicated using the *if* structure, the former often provides greater clarity. For example, suppose we wanted a program fragment that converts an integer in the range 0 . . 9 into word form. The *if* structure forces us to write something like

```
if DIGIT = 0 then
    PUT("zero");
elsif DIGIT = 1 then
    PUT("one");
elsif DIGIT = 2 then
    PUT("two");
elsif DIGIT = 3 then
    ...
end if;
```

Using a *case,* on the other hand, we can write

```
case DIGIT is
    when 0 => PUT("zero");
    when 1 => PUT("one");
    when 2 => PUT("two");
    ...
    when 9 => PUT("nine");
end case;
```

The list of choices must satisfy two requirements. First, the list must be exhaustive; i.e., every possible value of the expression must be accounted for. Second, no value can appear twice; i.e., each value can be associated with only one *when*. Ada permits an optional *others* clause to make the first requirement easier to meet. If *others* is used, it causes the corresponding statement to be executed for all values that do not occur elsewhere. The *others* clause must be placed at the end of the *case*. Here is a *case* structure that includes an *others* clause:

```
case QUANTITY/WEEKS is
    when 0,1 => PUT_LINE("Delivery date OK.");
                PRIORITY := 2;
    when 2,3 =>
                PUT_LINE("Date may conflict.");
                PRIORITY := 1;
    when others =>
                PUT_LINE("Date unacceptable.");
                PRIORITY := -1;
end case;
```

In some situations we do not wish a *case* to take any special action if the expression has a certain value. Since we cannot simply omit the value from the list of choices, Ada provides a statement called the *null* statement. When a null statement is encountered, it is ignored. Here is a *case* structure in which a null statement appears:

```
case PIECE_ID is
    when 1 => VALUE := 100;      --pawn
    when 2 => VALUE := 325;      --knight
    when 3 => VALUE := 350;      --bishop
    when 4 => VALUE := 500;      --rook
    when 5 => VALUE := 900;      --queen
    when 6 => null;              --king
    when others => PUT_LINE("Bad piece ID.");
end case;
```

The *if* and *case* structures obviously share a number of characteristics. First, they both allow a "default option" for unexpected values. *If* permits an *else,* while *case* permits an *others*. Second, they can both be viewed as "one in–one out" structures. That is, they are both organized to have only one entrance point and one exit point. When an *if* or a *case* is encountered, the first step is evaluation of the given expression. When an *if* or a *case* is completed, the last step is always a transfer of control to the statement that follows the structure.

2.3 LOOPING

A loop is a statement sequence that can be executed repetitively. A single pass through a loop is called an *iteration*. Ada provides several control structures for creating loops, of which the most basic is the *loop . . . exit* structure. To create a loop using this structure, we simply enclose a sequence of statements with the reserved words *loop* and *end loop*. One or more *exit* statements are then placed inside the loop to signal the conditions under which it terminates. Here is an example of such a loop:

```
loop
    DEGREES := DEGREES - 180;
    if DEGREES < 360 then
        exit;
    end if;
end loop;
```

When the *exit* statement is reached, the loop stops. Program execution then resumes at the point following the *end loop*. In this fragment, the iterations of the loop continue until DEGREES falls below 360. *Exit* also has an alternate form that allows us to omit the preceding *if*. An *exit* written in this form includes a boolean expression that signals the end of the loop. If the expression equals TRUE, the loop is terminated; otherwise, it continues. The loop presented above can be rewritten this way:

```
loop
    DEGREES := DEGREES - 180;
    exit when DEGREES < 360;
end loop;
```

The program shown in example 2.3 uses a loop to read a list of grades so it can compute their average. The value −1 is set aside by this program to indicate the end of the list. Since a grade is ordinarily a nonnegative value, one hopes, the use of −1 as a "stop code" should not endanger the integrity of the program. Notice that the *exit* in this loop appears in the middle, not at the end. A moment of inspection will show that this is necessary to prevent the stop code from making its way into the average.

Example 2.3

```
with TEXT_IO; use TEXT_IO;
procedure AVERAGE is
    STOP_CODE : constant INTEGER := -1;
    NEXT_NUMBER : INTEGER;
    SUM,COUNT : INTEGER := 0;
```

```
    package INT_IO is new INTEGER_IO(INTEGER);
    use INT_IO;
    --This program reads a list of grades and
    --finds their average. It continues to read
    --until it finds a number equal to STOP_CODE.
begin
    loop
        GET(NEXT_NUMBER);
        exit when NEXT_NUMBER = STOP_CODE;
        SUM := SUM + NEXT_NUMBER;
        COUNT := COUNT + 1;
    end loop;
    PUT(SUM/COUNT);
end AVERAGE;
```

The program shown in example 2.4 accepts a number and determines whether it is prime. Using the *rem* operator, it tests each integer between 2 and the number to see whether it can find a value that divides evenly. If such a factor is found, the loop terminates with FACTOR equal to the factor. If no factor is found, then the given number is prime, and the loop ends with FACTOR equal to the number. (The loop will not continue indefinitely, of course, because a number is always divisible by itself.)

Example 2.4

```
with TEXT_IO; use TEXT_IO;
procedure PRIME is
    NUMBER, FACTOR : INTEGER;
    package INT_IO is new INTEGER_IO(INTEGER);
    use INT_IO;
begin
    --read the number to be tested
    PUT_LINE("This program accepts a number and determines");
    PUT_LINE("whether it is prime.");
    PUT_LINE("Please enter the number.");
    GET(NUMBER);
    --is it prime?
    FACTOR := 1;
    loop
        FACTOR := FACTOR + 1;
        exit when NUMBER rem FACTOR = 0;
    end loop;
    --report the results
    if FACTOR = NUMBER then
        PUT_LINE("The number is prime.");
    else
        PUT("The number is divisible by");
        PUT(FACTOR);
    end if;
end PRIME;
```

In addition to the basic loop structure, Ada provides a variant called the *while* structure. When a *while* is encountered, its statement sequence is repeated as long as the specified boolean condition is true. Unlike the basic loop, in which testing of the termination condition may be deferred to the middle or the end of the sequence, a *while* always tests the boolean expression before the sequence is executed. Here is the general form of a *while* loop:

```
while boolean loop
     statement;
     statement;
     ...
     statement;
end loop;
```

Here is an example of a *while* loop:

```
while COUNT < 10 loop
    GET(NUMBER);
    SUM := SUM + NUMBER;
    COUNT := COUNT + 1;
end loop;
```

The *while* structure can be viewed as a formulation of a special case of the basic loop. For instance, the fragment above could be rewritten this way with the basic loop:

```
loop
    exit when COUNT < 10;
    GET(NUMBER);
    SUM := SUM + NUMBER;
    COUNT := COUNT + 1;
end loop;
```

The statement sequence within a loop can include another loop. An arrangement of this kind is called a *nested* loop. The program shown in example 2.5 uses a nested loop to print all the prime numbers within a user-specified range. The outer loop makes one iteration for each number in the range; the inner loop duplicates the function of the program in example 2.4.

Example 2.5

```
with TEXT_IO; use TEXT_IO;
procedure PRIME_LIST is
    LOWER, UPPER : INTEGER;        --range bounds
    FACTOR : INTEGER;              --tested divisor
    NUMBER : INTEGER;              --loop index
    package INT_IO is new INTEGER_IO(INTEGER);
    use INT_IO;
begin
    GET(LOWER);
    GET(UPPER);
    NUMBER := LOWER;
    while NUMBER <= UPPER loop
        FACTOR := 1
        loop
            FACTOR := FACTOR + 1;
            exit when NUMBER rem FACTOR = 0;
        end loop;
```

```
        if FACTOR = NUMBER then
            PUT(NUMBER);
        end if;
        NUMBER := NUMBER + 1;
    end loop;
end PRIME__LIST;
```

Now we face a question of semantics: does an *exit* in a nested loop leave the inner loop or the outer loop? The answer depends on the way the *exit* is written. In its default form, it terminates only the inner loop. Thus, in example 2.5, the *exit* causes the flow of control to resume with the *if* that follows the inner loop.

We can override this default by giving the outer loop a name. The name given to a loop can be any valid identifier. To assign a loop a name, we place it at the beginning and the end of the loop. (Its appearance at the beginning of the loop is punctuated by a colon.) An *exit* that specifies the name of a loop causes that loop to be terminated. Here is an example of a nested loop in which an *exit* is used to terminate the outer loop directly:

```
TABLE__LOOP:
    while ROWS < 10 loop
        while COLUMNS < 10 loop
            ...
            exit TABLE__LOOP;
            ...
        end loop;
    end loopTABLE__LOOP;
```

This form of *exit* can also be combined with its "conditional" form. If we wanted the outer loop in the fragment above to terminate when the quantity ROWS*COLUMNS exceeded 2E4, we could substitute the following:

```
exit TABLE__LOOP when ROWS*COLUMNS > 2E4;
```

Unlike identifiers for variables and constants, identifiers for loop names do not appear in the declarative part of the program. They are instead declared "implicitly" by their use.

2.4 COUNTED LOOPING

A counted loop is one designed to have a predetermined number of iterations. The outer loop in example 2.5 is a counted loop: it makes one iteration for every integer in the range LOWER . . UPPER. Loops of this kind appear often enough that Ada provides a control structure to handle them.

This structure is called the *for* loop. It is similar in form to the *while* loop. Instead of specifying only a boolean expression, however, the first line of a *for* loop specifies two components: a loop parameter and a range. The loop parameter is a variable whose value is maintained inside the loop. When a *for* is encountered, the loop parameter is set equal to the lower bound of the range. After each iteration of the loop, the value of the parameter is incremented. The loop terminates when the value of the parameter reaches the upper bound of the range. Here is the general form of a *for* loop:

```
for parameter in range loop
    statement;
    statement;
    ...
    statement;
loop end;
```

Although we obviously can devise a counted loop without using *for*, this new control structure is advantageous in several respects. First, it automatically initializes the loop parameter; second, it automatically increments the parameter; and finally, it makes the function of the loop more apparent. Here is a loop that prints the integers from one to ten:

```
for I in 1..10 loop
    PUT(I);
loop end;
```

Like a loop name, a loop parameter is declared implicitly. It is automatically given a data type corresponding to the type of the values in the range. Within the loop, it can be accessed by the program statements as if it were a constant. It can be printed and used in calculations, but it cannot be assigned a new value; the value can be changed only by the loop mechanism.

Example 2.6

```
with TEXT_IO; use TEXT_IO;
procedure MORE_PRIMES is
    LOWER,UPPER,FACTOR : INTEGER;
    package INT_IO is new INTEGER_IO(INTEGER);
    use INT_IO;
begin
    GET(LOWER);
    GET(UPPER);
    for NUMBER in LOWER..UPPER loop
        FACTOR := 2;
        while NUMBER rem FACTOR /= 0 loop
            FACTOR := FACTOR + 1;
        end loop;
        if NUMBER = FACTOR then
            PUT(NUMBER);
        end if;
    end loop;
end MORE_PRIMES;
```

The program shown in example 2.6 duplicates the program shown in example 2.5 using a *for* loop. No declaration for NUMBER is needed. Within the loop,

NUMBER successively takes on the values LOWER, LOWER + 1, LOWER + 2, and so on through UPPER. If LOWER and UPPER were given the same value, then the loop would have been executed exactly once before terminating. If LOWER were given a value greater than UPPER, then the loop would not have been executed at all. (A range of this kind is called a *null range*.)

Importantly, an identifier that names a loop parameter is not defined outside its loop. In this respect, a *for* loop can be viewed as having its own declarative part. The value of a loop parameter is therefore inaccessible after the loop has terminated.

Ada provides a variant of the *for* loop, the *for . . . reverse* loop, that causes the loop parameter to begin with the upper bound and work its way toward the lower bound. In this structure, the value of the loop parameter is decremented with each iteration rather than incremented. It has the same form as an ordinary *for* loop, except that the reserved word *reverse* follows the word *in*. The following loop counts from ten down to one:

```
for I in reverse 1..10 loop
    PUT(I);
end loop;
```

Exit statements can be embedded in a *for* loop to cause early termination. Like the other loop structures, *for* loops can be given names to allow termination from within a nested loop. As with normal termination of a *for* loop, early termination of a *for* loop leaves the loop parameter undefined.

2.5 EXCEPTIONAL TRANSFER

The control structures that we have seen thus far constitute a more than adequate selection for any process involving branches and loops. Nevertheless, Ada also provides a facility for performing *exceptional transfers*. An exceptional transfer causes the flow of control to jump from one arbitrarily chosen statement to another.

The destination of an exceptional transfer is marked with a *label*, which is an identifier enclosed by double angle brackets. Labels, like loop names, are declared implicitly. A single statement can be given more than one label. Here are some examples of labeled statements:

```
<<DONE>>end if;
<<REJECT>>PUT_LINE("Try again, please.");
<<DO_NOTHING>>null;
<<YES>><<OUI>><<SI>>Y:= Y + 1;
```

The initiation of an exceptional transfer is made by a *goto* statement. A *goto* causes program flow to jump to the statement with the specified label. In the following loop, a *goto* is used to emulate the unconditional form of *exit:*

```
while ROWS < 10 loop
    while COLUMNS < 10 loop
        ...
        goto TABLE_LOOP;
        ...
    end loop;
end loop;
<<TABLE_LOOP>>null;
```

Although the *goto* statement is more flexible than *exit,* which can be used only for loop termination, *goto* is subject to an important restriction: it cannot be used to jump into the middle of a "one in–one out" structure, such as an *if,* a *case,* or a *loop*. For this reason, the transfer made in the following fragment is invalid:

```
goto INSIDE_A_LOOP;
for I in reverse 2*WEIGHT..3*WEIGHT loop
    ...
    <<INSIDE_A_LOOP>>
    ...
end loop;
```

Moreover, an exceptional transfer cannot be used to make jumps from one part of a branching structure to another. Transfers can be made within a single statement sequence, of course, but they cannot be made between two statement sequences that correspond to different "branches." Here is an example of such a transfer:

```
if not DEVICE_WORKING then
    PUT_LINE("The device is not operational");
    goto READY_MESSAGE;
else
    PUT_LINE("The device is awaiting input");
    <<READY_MESSAGE>>
    PUT_LINE("Press any key when you are");
    PUT_LINE("ready to continue.");
end if;
```

Theoretical work has shown that exceptional transfers are inessential in a language that offers the other control structures presented in this chapter. Exceptional transfers should be avoided, in fact, because they often reduce program readability. Carelessly used, the *goto* statement can complicate a program enough that its flow of control becomes difficult to predict.

3

TYPE DECLARATIONS

3.1 ENUMERATION TYPES

Suppose we wanted to write a program to keep track of the days of the week. If we were restricted to using Ada's predeclared types, we might devise a scheme where the integer 0 stands for Sunday, 1 for Monday, 2 for Tuesday, and so on. To give TODAY the value "Thursday," we would then write

```
TODAY := 4;
```

This scheme is obviously a bit inconvenient; it requires us to make the mental effort of keeping the numerical codes straight. What we really want to write is

```
TODAY := THURSDAY;
```

What we want to do, in short, is to declare a new data type. Ada permits us to do just that. The declaration below defines a new type called DAYS whose values are days of the week:

```
type DAYS is (SUNDAY,MONDAY,TUESDAY,WEDNESDAY,THURSDAY,
              FRIDAY,SATURDAY);
```

DAYS is now a type identifier, like INTEGER and BOOLEAN. A variable of type DAYS can have any of the values listed in the declaration above. DAYS is an example of an *enumeration type*. An enumeration type is composed of a set of enumerated elements, which may be identifiers or character literals. Here are more declarations that create enumeration types:

```
type PLANETS is (MERCURY,VENUS,EARTH,MARS,JUPITER,SATURN,URANUS,
                 NEPTUNE,PLUTO);
type SEX is (MALE,FEMALE);
type HEX is ('0','1','2','3','4','5','6','7','8','9',A,B,C,D,E,F);
```

Having declared a type, we can declare variables of that type using its type identifier. (When a variable is given a programmer-defined type, the declaration of the variable cannot precede the declaration of the type.) Here is a declaration for a variable named TODAY of type DAYS:

```
TODAY : DAYS;
```

Having declared the variable, in turn, we can assign it a value, as below:

```
TODAY := THURSDAY;
```

We can also use it in boolean expressions:

```
if TODAY = WEDNESDAY then
    PUT_LINE("Reserve a cart and caddy.");
end if;
```

The other comparison operators can be used, too:

```
if TODAY < TUESDAY then
    PUT_LINE("...");
end if;
```

Comparisons involving enumeration types are determined by the ordering of the elements in the type declaration. The leftmost element in the declaration is the minimum value, while the rightmost is the highest value. For the type DAYS, this means that

```
SUNDAY < MONDAY < ... < FRIDAY < SATURDAY
```

Variables with enumeration types can be incorporated into Ada's other control structures, as well. Here is a *for* loop that "counts" from SATURN to PLUTO:

```
for OBJECT in SATURN .. PLUTO loop
    ...
end loop;
```

Within the loop, OBJECT takes the successive values SATURN, URANUS, NEPTUNE, and PLUTO. Here is a *case* that branches based on the current value of TODAY:

```
case TODAY is
    when SUNDAY,SATURDAY =>
            WEEKEND := TRUE;
    when MONDAY,TUESDAY,WEDNESDAY,
```

```
        THURSDAY,FRIDAY =>
            WEEKEND := FALSE ;
end case ;
```

The predefined type BOOLEAN is an enumeration type. It can be viewed as having this declaration:

```
type BOOLEAN is (FALSE,TRUE) ;
```

Elements of enumeration types can appear in more than one type declaration. An identifier or character literal that is included in more than one enumeration type is said to be *overloaded*. (Giving an identifier or a symbol multiple definitions like this is called *overloading*.) Here is a sequence of declarations in which the identifier DIAMONDS is overloaded:

```
type SUIT is (HEARTS,SPADES,CLUBS,DIAMONDS) ;
type GEMS is (RUBIES,EMERALDS,SAPPHIRES,DIAMONDS) ;
```

In most cases, the type of an overloaded enumeration element can be determined from the context of its usage. In a small number of instances, however, the type of an overloaded enumeration element may be ambiguous. An example of such an instance is a boolean expression in which a comparison has two overloaded operands. Another example is a specification for a loop parameter where the bounds of the range are both overloaded. In these cases, the overloaded entity must be *qualified*.

An enumeration element can be qualified by writing its type identifier, followed by a single quotation mark, followed by the element itself in parentheses. (The same form can be used to qualify any literal or expression in Ada.) Depending on the situation, we could qualify DIAMONDS in either of two ways:

```
SUIT'(DIAMONDS)
GEMS'(DIAMONDS)
```

Importantly, we need not qualify an entity except in a few unusual circumstances. For example, we could assign DIAMONDS to a variable of type SUIT or GEMS without qualifying it, because the data type of DIAMONDS could be inferred from the data type of the variable to which it is assigned. Likewise, we could use DIAMONDS as a choice in a *case* structure without qualifying it, because its data type could be inferred from the expression used to select the choices.

To perform input and output with enumeration types, we write an instantiation with the name ENUMERATION__IO. One instantiation is needed for each type that is involved in input–output. In a program that performs input and output for the types INTEGER, SUIT, and GEMS, a sequence of this kind should appear in the declarative part:

```
package INT__STUFF is new INTEGER__IO(INTEGER) ;
package SUIT__IO is new ENUMERATION__IO(SUIT) ;
```

```
package GEMS__IO is new ENUMERATION__IO(GEMS);
use INT__STUFF,SUIT__IO,GEMS__IO;
```

The identifiers INT__STUFF,SUIT__IO, and GEMS__IO were chosen arbitrarily. As noted in section 1.4, other identifiers could appear in the same place. GET and PUT can now be used with the given types. If an input value is an enumeration literal, no distinction is made between lower case and upper case letters.

3.2 SUBTYPES

Suppose we wanted a variable to store a quantity of change in cents. We know in advance that the value of this variable will always fall between 0 and 99. Ada allows us to incorporate this information into our program with a *subtype* declaration. Here is an example of a subtype declaration:

```
subtype CENTS is INTEGER range 0..99;
```

The declaration for CENTS specifies two pieces of information: a *base type* and a *constraint*. The base type of a subtype is simply the type whose values and operators it shares. Since the base type of CENTS is INTEGER, a variable of type CENTS can be assigned integer values and used in integer expressions. The constraint imposed on a subtype indicates the restrictions on its possible values. A variable of type CENTS has all the properties of a variable of type INTEGER, with one exception: it cannot be assigned a value outside the range 0..99.

A subtype declaration does not actually create a new type. A subtype is not considered distinct from its base type; as long as the constraints are obeyed, a subtype and its base type can be mixed in expressions and assignments. In fact, the constraint can be omitted altogether, in which case the subtype identifier is simply another name for the base type. The following declaration introduces the identifier WHOLE as a new name for the type INTEGER:

```
subtype WHOLE is INTEGER;
```

The base type can be an enumeration type. As usual, the enumeration type must be declared before the subtype. If DAYS has been declared as in section 3.1, we can declare a subtype of DAYS such as this one:

```
subtype WEEKDAYS is DAYS range MONDAY..FRIDAY;
```

The constraint imposed on a subtype must be compatible with any constraints on the base type. If we declared a subtype of WEEKDAYS, for instance, its range would have to lie within the range MONDAY . . FRIDAY. If we declared a subtype of CENTS, its range would have to lie within the range 0..99.

Example 3.1

```
with TEXT_IO; use TEXT_IO;
procedure LEAP_YEAR is
    subtype GREGORIAN is INTEGER range 1582..9999;
    YEAR : GREGORIAN;
    EXTRA_DAY : BOOLEAN;
    package INT_IO is new INTEGER_IO(INTEGER);
    use INT_IO;
begin
    GET(YEAR);
    EXTRA_DAY := FALSE;
    if (YEAR rem 4 = 0) and (YEAR mod 100 /= 0) then
        EXTRA_DAY := TRUE;
    elsif YEAR rem 400 = 0 then
        EXTRA_DAY := TRUE;
    end if;
    if EXTRA_DAY then
        PUT_LINE("The given year is a leap year.");
    else
        PUT_LINE("The given year is not a leap year.");
    end if;
end LEAP_YEAR;
```

The program shown in example 3.1 introduces a subtype of INTEGER whose possible values are dates of the Gregorian calendar. Since the bounds of a subtype need not be specified as literals, the declarations in this program might also have been written this way:

```
FIRST_YEAR : constant INTEGER := 1582;
LAST_YEAR : constant INTEGER := 9999;
subtype GREGORIAN is INTEGER range FIRST_YEAR..LAST_YEAR;
```

Subtypes can be defined implicitly in a variable declaration. Hence, we can impose a range constraint on a variable without writing a subtype declaration. Here is a declaration for an integer variable that cannot take values outside the range 32..212 :

```
for CHANGE in CENTS loop
    ...
end loop;
```

Subtypes can be defined implicitly in a variable declaration. Hence, we can impose a range constraint on a variable without writing a subtype declaration. Here is a declaration for an integer variable that cannot take values outside the range 32 . . 212 :

```
WATER_TEMP : INTEGER range 32..212;
```

Ada provides two predeclared subtypes of INTEGER called POSITIVE and NATURAL. A variable of type POSITIVE can have an integer value greater than zero. A variable of type NATURAL can have a value greater than or equal to zero.

The upper bounds of POSITIVE and NATURAL vary from one implementation of Ada to another.

3.3 DERIVED TYPES

Suppose we had a program in which some variables stored integer units of weight, say, while others stored integer units of temperature. In writing this program, we might give both groups of variables the data type INTEGER. Yet it seems odd to give them both the same data type when they are, in fact, logically distinct. The operations that we perform on units of weight are not logically related to the operations performed on units of temperature; it makes even less sense to mix the two kinds of data in arithmetic expressions. What can it mean to subtract "3 kilograms" from "10 degrees"? Obviously, it can mean nothing at all.

For this reason, Ada allows us to declare data types that are logically distinct, even though they may share the same literals and operators. These new types are called *derived types*. Here are two declarations that introduce a pair of derived types:

```
type KILOGRAMS is new INTEGER range 0..1e5;
type DEGREES is new INTEGER;
```

Derived type declarations are similar in form to subtype declarations. Just as a subtype has a base type, a derived type has a *parent type*. The types KILOGRAMS and DEGREES both have the parent type INTEGER. Additionally, the declaration for KILOGRAMS imposes a range constraint.

Unlike subtype declarations, however, derived type declarations introduce new and distinct types. KILOGRAMS and DEGREES are distinct both from INTEGER and from one another. As a consequence, values of type KILOGRAMS, DEGREES, and INTEGER cannot be mixed in expressions or assignments.

A derived type inherits the literals and operators that are defined for its parent type. These literals and operators are overloaded; their types are determined by context. To illustrate the relationships of overloaded operators across derived type boundaries, we will begin with the following declarations:

```
I1,I2,I3 : INTEGER;
K1,K2,K3 : KILOGRAMS;
D1,D2,D3 : DEGREES;
```

Having declared these variables as above, we can use them in expressions and assignments. The following examples show some legal and illegal assignments involving derived types:

```
I1 := I2 + 5;          --5 is of type INTEGER
K1 := K2 + 5;          --5 is of type KILOGRAMS
D1 := D2 + 5;          --5 is of type DEGREES
```

```
D2 := D2 - K3;           --illegal
I3 := D1 * D2;           --illegal
K2 := K2 + K1;           --of type KILOGRAMS
```

A derived type can, in turn, be the parent type of another derived type. Bearing in mind Ada's rule that identifiers cannot be used in advance of their declarations, we may write a sequence of declarations like this one:

```
type LENGTH is new INTEGER;
type INCHES is new LENGTH;
type METERS is new LENGTH;
```

In situations where we would like to override Ada's prohibition of type mixing, we can use the type conversion functions. For every derived type declaration, Ada produces two conversion functions: one converts values of the parent type into the derived type, while the other converts from the derived type to the parent. The name of the function is simply the identifier that names the "destination type" of the transfer. Here are some examples of assignments involving type conversion:

```
I1 := INTEGER(K2);                 --KILOGRAMS to INTEGER
I1 := INTEGER(D1*D2);              --DEGREES to INTEGER
K3 := K1 + KILOGRAMS(I3);          --INTEGER to KILOGRAMS
D3 := D1 * DEGREES(I1+I2);         --INTEGER to DEGREES
```

Type conversion funtions are not defined except for pairs of types such that one is the parent of the other. No function exists, for example, to convert directly from DEGREES to KILOGRAMS. This limitation is easily bypassed, however, because the result of one type conversion can be sent to another. Here are two assignments in which this kind of conversion is made:

```
D1 := DEGREES(INTEGER(K1));        --KILOGRAMS to DEGREES
K1 := KILOGRAMS(INTEGER(D1));      --DEGREES to KILOGRAMS
```

These conversions must, of course, satisfy any constraints that have been imposed on the types. If D1 had a value less than 0 or greater than 1e5, the second conversion above would fail. The inside conversion from DEGREES to INTEGER would succeed, but the outside conversion from INTEGER to KILOGRAMS would violate the latter's range constraint.

The parent type of a derived type need not be an integer type. Here are some derived type declarations in which other parent types appear:

```
type DECISION is new BOOLEAN;
type WORKDAYS is new DAYS range MONDAY..FRIDAY;
```

The declaration for WORKDAYS cannot be elaborated unless that for DAYS has been elaborated already. Since DAYS and WORKDAYS will be separate types, the enumeration elements in the range MONDAY . . FRIDAY will be overloaded.

Hence, it may occasionally be necessary to qualify them as described in the preceding section.

Since a derived type is distinct from its parent, we must write an instantiation for derived types that will be involved in input–output. The name of the derived type must appear in the instantiation. In a program that will perform input–output on values of type WORKDAYS, a line like this one should be included:

```
package WRK is new ENUMERATION__IO(WORKDAYS);
```

The name given in the instantiation—in this case, WRK—should also appear in a *use* clause. GET and PUT can then be used with the type. If an instantiation were provided only for the parent type, input–output facilities for the derived type would not be available.

3.4 TYPE ATTRIBUTES

Many processes that occur in a program can be coded in a way that is somewhat independent of the data type. For instance, suppose we want to write a loop that makes one iteration for each element of an enumeration type. Our first inclination would doubtless be to write the bounds of the loop parameter as a pair of literals, like this:

```
for STONE in RUBIES..DIAMONDS loop
    ...
loop end;
```

If we later redefine the enumeration type to include other elements, however, we might have to rewrite the loop to reflect the changes. Situations of this kind make it desirable to maintain a degree of independence between the body of a program, on one hand, and its type declarations, on the other. Ada promotes this goal by allowing programs to obtain information about type attributes.

An attribute inquiry is written by placing a type identifier in front of an attribute identifier, separating the two with an apostrophe. Two attributes that are defined for all the types we have used are FIRST and LAST. For a type named *T,* T'FIRST returns the minimum value in T and T'LAST returns the maximum value in T. We might, for example, replace the preceding loop with the following:

```
for STONE in GEMS'FIRST..GEMS'LAST loop
    ...
loop end;
```

An attribute identifier can also appear in the declarative part of a program. For instance, the predefined type POSITIVE mentioned in section 3.2 can be viewed as having the following declaration:

```
subtype POSITIVE is INTEGER range 1..INTEGER'LAST;
```

Some other attributes are SUCC, PRED, POS, and VAL. Among the types and subtypes we have seen so far, each have values with distinct *successors* and *predecessors*. The integer value 7 has the successor 8 and the predecessor 6. In the enumeration type (JAN,FEB,MARCH, . . . ,NOV,DEC), we can see that FEB has the successor MARCH and the predecessor JAN. (Of course, the minimum element of a type has no predecessor, and the maximum element has no successor.) SUCC and PRED return the successor and predecessor, respectively, of a given value in a given type. Thus,

```
INTEGER'SUCC(7) = 8
INTEGER'PRED(7) = 6
DAYS'SUCC(MONDAY) = TUESDAY
DAYS'PRED(MONDAY) = SUNDAY
```

Hence, although it is illegal to write

```
TOMORROW := TODAY + 1;
```

we can find the value of TOMORROW by writing

```
TOMORROW := DAYS'SUCC(TODAY);
```

Attempting to evaluate undefined expressions like DAYS'SUCC(SATURDAY) or GEMS'PRED(RUBIES) is invalid. We can make a type appear to "wrap around," however, with tests like this one:

```
if TODAY = SATURDAY then
    TOMORROW := SUNDAY;
else
    TOMORROW := DAYS'SUCC(TODAY);
end if;
```

Or, better yet,

```
if TODAY = DAYS'LAST then
    TOMORROW := DAYS'FIRST;
else
    TOMORROW := DAYS'SUCC(TODAY);
end if;
```

The types we have discussed so far have another distinguishing characteristic: each of their values has a unique *position number*. The position number of a value with an integer type or subtype is simply equal to itself. The position number of a value with an enumeration type is determined by the order of the elements in its declaration. In an enumeration type with *n* elements, the position numbers range from 0 to n − 1. The leftmost element has position number 0; the rightmost has position number n − 1. The attribute POS accepts a value and returns its position number:

```
INTEGER'POS(1e4) = 1e4
DAYS'POS(SATURDAY) = 6
DAYS'POS(DAYS'SUCC(MONDAY)) = 3
GEMS'POS(RUBIES) = 0
```

The attribute VAL, on the other hand, accepts an integer expression representing a position number and returns the corresponding element in the type. An error condition occurs if the position number is not valid for the type. So,

```
INTEGER'VAL(1e4) = 1e4
DAYS'VAL(6) = SATURDAY
GEMS'VAL(0) = RUBIES
```

The data types that we have examined up to this point form a category of types called *discrete types*. The data types INTEGER and BOOLEAN are discrete types, as are their subtypes and derived types. Enumeration types fall into this category as well. The distinction between discrete types and nondiscrete types is important in many areas. The range of a *for* loop must have a discrete type; the same is true of a *case* selector. In addition, the attributes SUCC, PRED, POS, and VAL are defined only for discrete types.

4

OTHER NUMERIC TYPES

4.1 FLOATING POINT TYPES

To allow manipulations of noninteger quantities, Ada provides two representations for real numbers. In this section we examine floating point types; in the subsequent section we examine fixed point types. Although they are not discrete types, they share a broader category with discrete types: real types and discrete types, taken together, are called *scalar types*.

The rules for writing real number literals are the same as those for integer literals, with two exceptions: first, a real literal includes a decimal point, and second, a real literal can have a negative exponent part. (The decimal point must be enclosed by at least one digit on both sides.) Here are some examples of real literals:

```
0.0
3.14159
-1.3
6.02e+23
```

All of the boolean comparison operators are available for use with real values. The symbols are defined as they are for the type INTEGER. Both operands of a boolean comparison must have the same type. The membership operators can also be used to determine whether a real value lies within a given real subtype. Here are some boolean expressions that involve real numbers:

```
MASS < 0.99
(X /= 0.0) and (X /= 1.0)
ANGLE in 0.0 .. 180.0
```

We declare a floating point type by specifying its minimal precision and, optionally, its range constraint. The precision is the number of decimal digits of accuracy that must be maintained when a value of the type is stored. The range constraint, if one appears, is the same as with integer types: it indicates the range of values that the type will permit. Here are some examples of floating point type declarations:

```
type REAL is digits 8 ;
type FLOATER is digits 9 range -10__000.0 .. +10__000.0 ;
type MONEY is digits 8 range LOWER..UPPER ;
```

A subtype or derived type of a floating point type must be compatible with the parent type. In particular, the new type cannot extend outside the limits imposed by the parent type in terms of either its accuracy or its range. Here are some declarations based on the declarations above:

```
subtype SMALL__REAL is REAL digits 7 ;
type NEW__FLOATER is new FLOATER digits 5 ;
type BALANCE is new MONEY digits 8 range 0.0..UPPER;
```

Except for *mod* and *rem,* which are not available for noninteger types, floating-point expressions can include any of the operations available in integer expressions. An overloaded arithmetic operator that is given floating-point operands returns a floating point result. Unlike integer division, which yields only the integer part of the quotient, floating point division returns the fractional part as well. Hence,

```
9/4 = 2
9.0/4.0 = 2.25
```

The predefined binary operators cannot be given operands with different types. (An exception is the exponentiation operator, whose right operand must be an integer, regardless of the type of its left operand.) Unless explicit type conversions are made, integer and floating point operands cannot be mixed; floating point operands having different types cannot be mixed, either. Conversions between numeric types, as discussed in section 3.3, can be accomplished by preceding an expression with the identifier that names the "target" type and separating the two with an apostrophe. To illustrate numeric type conversion, we will begin with these declarations:

```
TIPS : MONEY ;
INCOME : SMALL__REAL ;
P,Q : INTEGER ;
```

Here are some assignments that make conversions between floating point types:

```
INCOME := 2.0 * SMALL__REAL'(TIPS) ;
TIPS := TIPS + MONEY'(INCOME)/3 ;
```

No conversion is necessary, of course, if one of the types is a subtype of the other; conversion is required only if the types we want to mix are distinct. Conversion from an integer type to a floating point type yields a simple mapping of values, like so:

```
INCOME := SMALL_REAL'(-1);        --equals -1.0
TIPS := MONEY'(5);                --equals 5.0
```

Conversion from a floating point type to an integer type is done with rounding, like so:

```
P := INTEGER'(-1.0);        --equals -1
Q := INTEGER'(3.14);        --equals 3
```

A predeclared floating point type called FLOAT is provided. Its characteristics are dependent on the Ada implementation. We can use attribute enquiries to determine these characteristics. The attribute identifiers FIRST and LAST are defined for all scalar types; in addition, the attribute DIGITS is defined for real types. DIGITS returns an integer that indicates the minimal accuracy of the type in decimal digits. Thus, we can determine the accuracy of FLOAT with the expression FLOAT'DIGITS.

To perform input–output with floating point types, we write an instantiation using FLOAT_IO. One instantiation is needed for each floating point type that will be involved in input–output. In a program that performs input–output on values of type FLOAT and of type BALANCE, we write

```
package FL_IO is new FLOAT_IO(FLOAT);
package BAL_IO is new FLOAT_IO(BALANCE);
use FL_IO,BAL_IO;
```

GET and PUT can now be used with these types. By default, PUT displays floating point numbers in scientific notation. Section 4.4 describes how to specify alternate formats.

4.2 FIXED POINT TYPES

The principal difference between floating point types and fixed point types is that the accuracy of a fixed point type is specified as an absolute figure called its *delta*. The delta of a fixed point type is an upper bound on its representational error. A fixed point type having a delta of 0.001, for example, represents all the numbers inside its range constraint with an inprecision of no more than plus or minus 0.001. Here are some declarations for fixed point types:

```
type SMALL__FIXED is delta 1.0e - 3 range 0.0 .. 1.0;
type INACCURATE is delta 10.0 range - 100.0 .. 100.0;
type BOUNDED is delta MAX__ERROR range - 127.0 .. 128.0;
```

Both the delta and the range must be specified for a fixed point type. The set of arithmetic operators available with fixed point types is similar to that available for the other numeric types. The following table shows the overloaded operators that are available for fixed point types:

Operator	Operands
+, -, abs	fixed (unary)
+, -	fixed and fixed
*,/	fixed and fixed
*	fixed and integer
*	integer and fixed
/	fixed and integer

For addition and subtraction, the usual rules of type consistency are maintained: these operators cannot be operands with different fixed point types. For multiplication and division, however, the rules are not maintained. First, these operators can be given operands with two different fixed point types, in which case they return a fixed-point value. This value is not initially associated with a particular type; it can be converted into a "named" type with an explicit conversion.

Second, these operators allow limited mixing of integer and real operands. When a value with a fixed point type is multiplied or divided by a value of type INTEGER, the result has the same fixed-point type. (Note that the exponentiation operator is unavailable for fixed point types.)

Example 4.1

```
with TEXT__IO; use TEXT__IO;
procedure CIRCLE is
    type MY__FIXED is delta 0.0001 range 0.0 .. 1.0e5;
    PI : constant MY__FIXED := 3.1415;
    CIRCUMFERENCE,AREA : MY__FIXED;
    RADIUS : NATURAL;
    package MY__IO is new FIXED__IO(MY__FIXED);
    use MY__IO;
begin
    GET (RADIUS);
    CIRCUMFERENCE := 2*PI*RADIUS;
    AREA := PI * RADIUS ** 2;
    PUT(AREA);
    PUT(CIRCUMFERENCE);
end CIRCLE;
```

The program shown in example 4.1 offers a simple demonstration of type mixing in expressions. (Note that an instantiation is written for MY __FIXED using FIXED__IO.) The expression in the first assignment is evaluated left to right, in accordance with precedence rules. Both multiplications in the expression take an integer and a fixed point number; the expression returns a value of type MY__FIXED. The expression in the second assignment is evaluated from right to left, of course, because exponentiation has higher precedence than multiplication. The exponentiation returns an integer value, which is then multiplied by a fixed point value to return a fixed point value. These assignments succeed because both sides are of type MY__FIXED; if PI were given a different fixed-point type, the results of the expressions would not be compatible with CIRCUMFERENCE and AREA.

Along with FIRST and LAST, which are available for all scalar types, some attributes available for fixed point types include DELTA and MACHINE__ROUNDS. The first returns the delta specified in the type declaration. The second returns a boolean value indicating whether results of fixed point arithmetic are rounded or truncated. For any fixed point type F, the attribute enquiry F'MACHINE__ROUNDS returns TRUE if rounding is performed. If not, then any part of a result that lies outside the precision specified by the delta is discarded.

4.3 BASED NUMBERS

In general practice we will write numeric literals in decimal form—that is, in base 10. We can, however, write numbers in other bases. Ada permits numeric literals to take the form of *based numbers,* which can be written in any base from binary (base 2) to hexadecimal (base 16).

To write an integer as a based number, we write the base followed by the number itself, which is enclosed by pound signs. Underscores may be included for clarity, as with conventional literals. Here are some based numbers that represent the decimal integer 127:

```
2#1111111#
2#111__1111#
8#177#
10#127#
```

To write in bases above 10, we must have additional digits. Ada uses the letters A through F for this purpose. The letter A stands for 10, B for 11, and so on. Here are some based numbers written in hexadecimal:

```
16#8#        --equals 8
16#F#        --equals 15
16#f#        --equals 15
16#10#       --equals 16
16#7F#       --equals 127
```

Based numbers can include an exponent part. If an exponent is included, it is preceded by a letter E, as usual. The exponent is written in decimal. When a based number is encountered in a program, it is multiplied by the value of the base raised to the power of the exponent. Here are some based numbers that have exponent parts:

```
16#7F#e0        --equals 127
16#7F#e1        --equals 127*16, or 2032
10#12#e4        --equals 12e4, or 120000
8#1#E+4         --equals 1*(8**4), or 4096
2#111#e3        --equals 7*(2**3), or 56
```

Real based numbers are distinguished by the inclusion of a decimal point. Assuming that X and Y are declared to be floating point or fixed point variables, the following assignments are valid:

```
X:= 16#7F.0#;           --equals 127.0
Y:= 16#7.F#e1;          --equals 127.0
X:=2#0.1#;              --equals 0.5
Y:=2#0.1#E2;            --equals 2.0
X:=10#3.0#;             --equals 3.0
Y:=10#314#e - 2;        --equals 3.14
```

Certain bases, such as binary and hexadecimal, are often used to write device-dependent values such as status codes or memory addresses. These bases are preferred over decimal in many instances because binary and hexadecimal numbers are easier for a programmer to convert into the internal form by which integers are represented. Considerations of this kind do not arise in the development of most programs, however; the conventional decimal form that we have been using is generally the notation of choice.

4.4 FORMATTING NUMERIC OUTPUT

Each numeric type has a default output format. These defaults are defined by the Ada implementation. We can override them, however, by instructing PUT to use other formats.

For integer values, we can specify the output width and the output base. The output width is the minimum number of characters that the value will occupy. If a value requires fewer characters, extra blanks will be added on its left. Suppose the default width is 6. Then the statement PUT(33) will print *33* preceded by four padding blanks. If a value requires more characters, on the other hand, then the minimum width will be ignored.

The default base is 10. If the default is overridden, the output value will appear as a based number. To specify another base, we provide a value of the predefined type NUMBER__BASE. This type is implicitly declared as a subtype of INTEGER:

```
subtype NUMBER__BASE is INTEGER range 2..16;
```

Here are some integer PUT statements for which the output format is partially or fully specified:

```
PUT(I*J, WIDTH => 1);                      --base is default
PUT(abs(I**2 - J**2), BASE => 8);          --width is default
PUT(K,WIDTH => 4,BASE => 2);
PUT(K,BASE => 2,WIDTH => 4);               --same as above
```

The format of fixed point and floating point types is specified with three values. The first is called FORE; it gives the minimum number of characters allocated to the integer part of the number. The second is called AFT; it gives the minimum number of characters allocated to the fractional part of the number. The third is called EXP; it gives the number of characters allocated to the exponent part. (A sign is always included in the exponent part.)

If fewer than FORE digits are needed to the left of the decimal point, leading blanks are added. If fewer than AFT digits are needed to the right of the decimal point, trailing zeros are added. If fewer than EXP-1 digits are needed for the exponent, leading zeros are added. If EXP is zero, then the number is printed in conventional form without an exponent part.

The examples below illustrate different formats. A *b* is used to indicate a blank.

```
PUT(12.0,FORE=>3, AFT=>3,EXP=>0);          --b12.000
PUT(12.0,FORE=>4, AFT=>2,EXP=>0);          --bb12.00
PUT(12.0,FORE=>1, AFT=>1,EXP=>0);          --12.0
PUT(12.0,FORE=>4, AFT=>2,EXP=>3);          --bbb1.20E+01
PUT(1.2,FORE=>4, AFT=>2,EXP=>3);           --bbb1.20E+00
PUT(-12.03,FORE=>4, AFT=>1,EXP=>0);        --b-12.0
PUT(-12.07,FORE=>4, AFT=>1,EXP=>0);        --b-12.1
PUT(1/2,FORE=>3, AFT=>3,EXP=>2);           --bb5.000E-1
```

As the fourth and fifth examples show, the integer part of a number in exponential form is reduced to one digit. The value of the exponent is adjusted accordingly. As the sixth and seventh examples show, the last digit of the fractional part is rounded if necessary.

For floating point types, the default FORE is 2 and the default EXP is 3. The default AFT is defined by the implementation. For fixed point types, the default EXP is 0, with both FORE and AFT defined by the implementation.

Attributes named FORE and AFT are provided. They accept an identifier for a fixed point type and return the corresponding default. If the default FORE is 3, and MY__FIXED is a fixed point type, then the inquiry MY__FIXED'FORE returns 3.

5

ARRAYS

5.1 CONSTRAINED ARRAY DECLARATIONS

Unlike a scalar type, which can represent only one value, a *composite* type can represent a collection of values. One variety of composite types provided by Ada is the *array*. A variable having an array type can store a collection of homogeneous values, referred to as its *components*. They are homogeneous in the sense that they all have the same data type. This type is called the *component type* of the array. Here is a declaration for an array variable:

```
SALES : array(1 .. 7) of FLOAT ;
```

SALES is an array with seven components. Since this array has the component type FLOAT, each of its components can be used like a variable of type FLOAT. The first component is accessed as SALES(1), the second as SALES(2), and so on. Here is a loop that sets all the components of SALES equal to zero:

```
for I in 1 .. 7 loop
    SALES(I) := 0.0 ;
end loop ;
```

The value used to specify a component of an array is called its *index*. The declaration for an array indicates both its component type and its index types. The index type of SALES is a subtype of INTEGER. An array can have any number of index types; however, they must all be discrete types. (No restrictions apply to the component type.) Here are some additional array declarations:

```
MAX_TEMPS : array(JAN .. DEC,1 .. 31) of DEGREES ;
GRADES : array(1 .. STUDENTS) of INTEGER ;
CUBE : array(1 .. 3,1 .. 3,1 .. 3) of BOOLEAN ;
```

The following assignments give values to components of these arrays:

```
SALES(1) := 2.0e3;
MAX__TEMPS(MARCH,3) := 50;
GRADES(7) := 89;
CUBE(3,2,1) := TRUE;
```

Type identifiers can be used to indicate the index types in an array declaration. Also, an array type declaration can be elaborated in a type declaration as well as in a variable declaration. The following series of declarations shows these options in use:

```
type SUIT is (CLUBS,HEARTS,SPADES,DIAMONDS);
type FACE__VALUE is INTEGER range 2..14;
type DECK is array(SUIT,FACE__VALUE) of BOOLEAN;
HAVE__CARD : DECK;
```

HAVE__CARD is a variable of type DECK. It has fifty-two components of type BOOLEAN. One of the advantages of introducing a type identifier for an array type is that we can manipulate variables with the same type more easily than variables with different types. Consider the following declarations:

```
type LIST is array(1..20) of INTEGER;
P : LIST;
Q : LIST;
P1 : array(1..20) of INTEGER;
Q1 : array(1..20) of INTEGER;
```

P and Q have the same type. P1 and Q1, however, are associated with different type declarations and hence have different types. Thus, to copy the contents of P1 onto Q1, we would have to write

```
for I in 1..20 loop
    Q1(I) := P1(I);
end loop;
```

In contrast, Ada allows two arrays of the same type to be copied with a single assignment. So we can copy P onto Q by writing

```
Q := P;
```

Two arrays of the same type can also be compared using the boolean comparison operators. The equality and inequality operators perform a component-by-component test. If every component in P is equal to its corresponding component in Q, then the two arrays are considered equal. The following *if* performs such a test:

```
if P = Q then
    TEMP := P(1);      --interchange P(1) and P(2)
    P(1) := P(2);
    P(2) := TEMP;
end if;
```

The other comparison operators are available only for arrays with a discrete component type. Array comparisons start with the first pair of components; if that pair is equal, the comparison advances to the next pair, and so on. Suppose we begin with these declarations:

```
A,B,C,D : array(1 .. 3) of NATURAL ;
```

Suppose, also, that the arrays have the values shown in the following table:

	(1)	(2)	(3)
A	3	3	3
B	3	4	0
C	3	2	0
D	5	1	0

The order of the arrays, from smallest to largest, is C<A<B<D. Consequently, these array relations will return TRUE:

```
D > A
C < B
B /= A
```

An array with boolean components can be used as an operand for logical operators. The operators *and, or,* and *xor* accept a pair of boolean arrays with matching components. The specified operation is performed on matching components of the two arrays; another boolean array is returned. The *not* operator, similarly, accepts an array of boolean components and returns an array of components with the inverse boolean values.

If the bounds of an index type are indicated with integer literals, then the index type is assumed to be a subtype of INTEGER. To use a different integer type as an index type, we must give its name in the array declaration. The following declaration defines an array that can be indexed with values of type HOURS:

```
OVERTIME : array(HOURS range 1 .. 40) of FLOAT ;
```

The component type of an array can be another array. In this case, Ada allows us to access the array on three levels: by the value of the entire array, by the value of a component array, and by the value of a component of the component array. Suppose we begin with the following declaration:

```
TABLE : array(1 .. 5) of LIST ;
```

TABLE can be viewed as having five components of type LIST or one hundred components of type INTEGER. To access a single component of type LIST, say the first, we write

```
TABLE(1)
```

To access a component of that array, in turn, we must provide an additional index. We can access the fifth component of the first array in TABLE by writing

```
TABLE(1)(5)
```

Note that this notation is distinct from that used for multidimension arrays. If TABLE2 were declared as *array(1 . . 5,1 . . 20) of INTEGER*, it would have one hundred components, but it would not be an array of arrays. We would therefore use a notation like

```
TABLE2(1,5)
```

No limit is placed on the number of indices that an array can be given. The number of indices given to an array is called its *dimensionality*. The array TABLE has one dimension, while TABLE2 has two.

Example 5.1

```
with TEXT_IO; use TEXT_IO;
procedure STATS is
    MAX_SIZE : constant INTEGER := 100;
    type LIST is array(1..MAX_SIZE) of FLOAT;
    LIST_SIZE : INTEGER range 1..MAX_SIZE;
    SAMPLES : LIST;
    AVERAGE,VARIANCE : FLOAT := 0.0;
    package INT_IO is new INTEGER_IO(INTEGER);
    package FLT_IO is new FLOAT_IO(FLOAT);
    use INT_IO,FLT_IO;
begin
    --Read the list
    PUT_LINE("How many samples are in your list?");
    GET(LIST_SIZE);
    NEW_LINE;
    PUT_LINE("Please enter the samples.");
    for I in 1..LIST_SIZE loop
        GET(SAMPLES(I));
    end loop;
    --Find the average
    for I in 1..LIST_SIZE loop
        AVERAGE := AVERAGE + SAMPLES(I);
    end loop;
    AVERAGE := AVERAGE/LIST_SIZE;
    --Find the variance
    for I in 1..LIST_SIZE loop
        VARIANCE := VARIANCE + (SAMPLES(I)-AVERAGE)**2;
    end loop;
    VARIANCE := VARIANCE/LIST_SIZE;
    --Print the results
    PUT("The average of these samples is");
    PUT(AVERAGE);
    NEW_LINE;
    PUT("The variance of these samples is");
    PUT(VARIANCE);
end STATS;
```

The program shown in example 5.1 accepts a collection of floating point numbers and places them in an array. Since the upper bound of LIST is MAX_SIZE, and MAX_SIZE equals 100, up to 100 numbers can be accepted. Once the list is finished, the program calculates the average and the variance of the numbers. LIST_SIZE stores the number of array components that will be needed. The loops have the range 1 . . LIST_SIZE so that "empty" components are not included in the calculations.

5.2 UNCONSTRAINED ARRAY DECLARATIONS

The array types presented in the previous section were all "constrained" in the sense that the bounds of the index types were provided in the type declarations. Having declared a constrained array type, we cannot declare variables of that type with differing sizes. In many programs, however, we will want to create arrays whose index bounds are not known in advance. Ada therefore provides a facility for unconstrained array types, whose bounds need not be determined at the time the type is introduced.

The form of an unconstrained array declaration is the same as that of a constrained declaration, except that the two-character symbol "<>" is used in place of an explicit range indication. This symbol is called a *box;* it indicates that the actual range will be provided later. Here are some examples of unconstrained array types:

```
type HEIGHTS is array(INTEGER range <>) of FLOAT;
type BIT_MAP is array(INTEGER range <>) of BOOLEAN;
type MATRIX is array(XTYPE range <>,YTYPE range <>) of FLOAT;
```

A variable cannot be associated directly with an unconstrained array type. A subtype of the unconstrained type must be defined first; the subtype imposes the subscript bounds. Here are some declarations for subtypes of HEIGHTS:

```
subtype FEW is HEIGHTS(1..5);
subtype MANY is HEIGHTS(1..100);
subtype MOST is HEIGHTS(-1000..1000);
```

The first declaration defines an array subtype with five components of type FLOAT; the second defines a subtype with one hundred components; and the third defines a subtype with 2001 components. Variables given these subtypes will share the base type HEIGHTS. Array subtype definitions can also be made implicitly in a variable declaration, as below:

```
H1 : HEIGHTS(1..5);
H2, H3 : HEIGHTS(-5..0);
M1 : MATRIX(1..10,1..20);
B1 : BIT_MAP(0..15);
```

These variables are now associated with unconstrained array types. The bounds imposed by a subtype of an unconstrained array type (whether defined implicitly or explicitly) are called the *index constraints* of the subtype. The only restriction on index constraints is that they must be compatible with the index type named in the declaration of the base type. For subtypes of HEIGHTS and BIT__MAP, the index constraint must be a discrete range of INTEGER. For MATRIX, the two index constraints must be discrete ranges of XTYPE and YTYPE respectively.

Assignments between arrays having the same base type are possible even if the two arrays have different index constraints. The arrays must have the same number of components in each dimension, however. Arrays that meet this requirement are considered to have matching components. Recall that only boolean arrays with matching components can be evaluated with the logical operators. These declarations form a pair of boolean arrays with matching components:

```
BITS : BIT__MAP(1..8);        --eight components
BYTE : BIT__MAP(0..7);        --eight components
```

BITS and BYTE can be mixed in assignments as below:

```
BITS := BYTE;
BITS := not BYTE;
BITS := BITS or BYTE;
```

These declarations create a pair of two-dimensional arrays with matching components:

```
subtype BOARD is MATRIX(1..10,1..10);
SQUARE1 : BOARD;
SQUARE2 : MATRIX(21..30,2001..2010);
```

Arrays with different index constraints can also be mixed in comparisons. As usual, the arrays must have a discrete component type. If all other things are equal, the shorter array (that is, the array with fewest components) is considered the smallest. In this respect, the relational order of arrays is analogous to that of words in a dictionary.

To determine the bounds of an array variable, we can use the four attributes that Ada provides for arrays. Unlike most attributes, array attribute inquiries are defined both for type identifiers and for variable identifiers. The attributes FIRST(n) and LAST(n) return the lower and upper bounds of the n-th index of the given variable or type. Here are some inquiries formed with these attributes:

```
H1'FIRST(1)    --equals 1
H1'LAST(1)     --equals 5
M1'FIRST(1)    --equals 1
M1'LAST(1)     --equals 10
M1'LAST(2)     --equals 20
```

The attribute LENGTH(n) returns an integer corresponding to the number of values possible for the n-th index. If the index is a null range, then LENGTH returns 0. Here are some inquiries formed with LENGTH:

```
H2'LENGTH(1)        --equals 6
M1'LENGTH(1)        --equals 10
B1'LENGTH(1)        --equals 16
MANY'LENGTH(1)      --equals 100
```

The attribute RANGE(n) yields the discrete range corresponding to the n-th index. In other words, for an array type or variable named X, the inquiry X'RANGE(I) gives the subtype whose range is X'FIRST(I) . . X'LAST(I). Here is a *for* loop that uses this attribute to find the sum of all the components in a one-dimensional array named SALES:

```
SUMS := 0.0;
for K in SALES'RANGE(1) loop
    SUMS := SUMS + SALES(K);
end loop;
```

Here is a similar loop that works with a two-dimensional array named EARNINGS:

```
SUMS := 0.0;
for I in EARNINGS'RANGE(1) loop
    for J in EARNINGS'RANGE(2) loop
        SUMS := SUMS + EARNINGS(I,J);
    end loop;
end loop;
```

The "subscript" that specifies the index can be omitted from these attribute inquiries. If no index number is provided, then the attribute is applied to the first index by default. Thus, EARNINGS'FIRST is the same as EARNINGS'FIRST(1), EARNINGS'RANGE is the same as EARNINGS'RANGE(1), and so on.

5.3 AGGREGATES AND SLICES

Suppose we have an array with six components of type INTEGER. Suppose, also, that we want to assign its components the values 2, 4, 6, 8, 10, and 12 respectively. At this point, we have two means for placing values in such an array: we can assign it the value of another array or we can assign it values one component at a time. The first method is clearly inappropriate in this instance, while the second is manifestly cumbersome. To perform this array assignment, we must write a sequence like this:

```
HOURS(1) := 2;
HOURS(2) := 4;
```

```
HOURS(3) := 6;
HOURS(4) := 8;
HOURS(5) := 10;
HOURS(6) := 12;
```

A slightly more clever approach can bring us greater concision, though arguably at the expense of clarity:

```
for I in 1..6 loop
    HOURS(I) := 2*I;
loop end;
```

Needless to say, we cannot always count on a rescue from clever approaches. Ada provides a lexical entity called the *array aggregate* so we can write array values just as we write scalar values. Two kinds of aggregates are available: *positional* and *name*. A positional array aggregate is written as a list of values enclosed in parentheses, as in this assignment:

```
HOURS := (2,4,6,8,10,12);
```

The first value in the list is assigned to the component with the lowest index; the second value is assigned to the next lowest component; and so on. The number of components accounted for in the aggregate must equal the number of components in the array. Here are some other assignments written with positional aggregates:

```
PSW := (TRUE,TRUE,FALSE,TRUE);       --four boolean components
VECTOR := (1.0,-1.0);                --two real components
PALETTE := (RED,RED,GREEN);          --three components, enumeration type
```

A name aggregate is written as a list of indices or index ranges, each of which is followed by the value that the specified components will take. Here are some examples of name aggregates:

```
HOURS := (1..6 => 0);
HOURS := (1..3 => 0, 4..6 => 1);
HOURS := (1 => -3, 2..5 => -4, 6 => -3);
```

In the first example, HOURS(1) through HOURS(6) are set to 0. In the second example, HOURS(1) through HOURS(3) are set to 0, while HOURS(4) through HOURS(6) are set to 1. In the third example, HOURS(1) is set to −3, HOURS(2) through HOURS(5) are set to −4, and HOURS(6) is set to −3. If several components are to be given the same value, and the components do not have indices that fall in a continuous range (like 1 . . 3 or 1 . . 6), the aggregate can be abbreviated. A vertical bar (|) can be used to show that more than one index or index range is to be assigned a value. For instance, the third assignment above can be rewritten this way:

```
HOURS := (1|6 => -3, 2..5 => -4);
```

Here is an assignment that gives alternate components of HOURS the values −1 and −2 respectively:

```
HOURS := (1|3|5 => -1, 2|4|6 => -2);
```

The reserved word *others* can be used to indicate that a certain value should be assigned to all the components that are not otherwise referenced in the aggregate. If an *others* clause appears in an aggregate, it must be the last entry. (In most cases, an aggregate with an *others* clause must be qualified with a type identifier, as discussed in section 3.1). Assuming that HOURS is of type SIX__NUMS, the following pair of assignments will have identical effects:

```
HOURS := SIX__NUMS'(1|6 => -3, others => -4);
HOURS := SIX__NUMS'(2..5 => -4, others => -3);
```

To write an aggregate for an array of more than one dimension, we simply write an aggregate whose components are themselves aggregates. Suppose we have an array declared as follows:

```
SQUARE : array(1..3,1..3) of NATURAL;
```

Here are three assignments that sets all the components of equal SQUARE to 1:

```
SQUARE := ((1,1,1), (1,1,1), (1,1,1);       --positional
SQUARE := (1..3 => (1,1,1));                --name + positional
SQUARE := (1..3 => (1..3 => 1));            --name
```

As discussed in section 1.3, constants and variables can be given initial values when they are declared. Aggregates can be used in array declarations to give an array an initial value. Assuming that the type identifiers HEIGHTS, BIT__MAP, and MATRIX have been declared as in section 5.2, we can write declarations like

```
H4 : HEIGHTS(5..7) := (6.0,6.1,6.2);
B6 : constant BIT__MAP(0..63) := (0..31 => TRUE, 32..63 => FALSE;
M9 : constant MATRIX(1..2,1..2) := ((1.0,2.0),(3.0,4.0));
```

At this point we have seen the facilities that Ada provides for making assignments to a single component of an array and for making assignments to an entire array. But we are not yet able to make an assignment to a portion of an array without writing a sequence of individual assignments. To set the first three components of HOURS to 0, for instance, we must write

```
HOURS(1) := 0;
HOURS(2) := 0;
HOURS(3) := 0;
```

A contiguous portion of a single-dimension array, such as HOURS(1) through HOURS(3), is called a *slice*. Ada lets us manipulate slices as easily as entire arrays.

To reference a slice, we write its subscript range where we ordinarily write a single subscript. The following assignment duplicates the assignments in the preceding sequence:

```
HOURS(1..3):= (0, 0, 0);
```

This assignment places 1 in each component of the slice HOURS(4 . . 5):

```
HOURS(4..5):= (1, 1);
```

Slices with matching components can be mixed in assignments and comparisons. (Slices meet this rule only if they have the same base type and the same number of components.) Suppose we start with these declarations:

```
B7: BIT__MAP(-6..0);
B9: BIT__MAP(1..9);
```

These assignments are valid:

```
B7(-6..-3):= B9(2..5);
B9(1..3):= B7(-2..0);
B7(-6..-4):= B7(-3..-1);
B9(1..4):= B9(6..9);
```

These assignments are invalid:

```
B7(-1..0):= B9(1..3);
B9(2..4):= B9(5..9);
```

We must distinguish between a *component* of an array and a *one-component slice*. A component of an array, such as HOURS(2), has a data type that is different from the type of a slice like HOURS(2 . . 2). The type of an array component, of course, is simply the component type of the array. The type of an array slice, on the other hand, is the base type of the array. If HOURS is of type SIX__NUMS and it has the component type INTEGER, then

```
HOURS(2)        --is of type INTEGER
HOURS(2..2)     --is of type SIX__NUMS
```

Assignments involving two slices of the same array can be made, as shown in the examples. The two slices can overlap, if desired. Since the expression on the right-hand side of an assignment operator is evaluated before the assignment begins, an assignment with overlapping slices is not ambiguous. Say that HOURS has the value (1,2,3,4,5,6) when this assignment is encountered:

```
HOURS(2..5):= HOURS(3..6);
```

Following the assignment, HOURS will have the contents (1,3,4,5,6,6). Though slice operations cannot be performed on multidimension arrays, they can be performed on arrays with array components. Recall these declarations from the first section of this chapter:

```
type LIST is array(1 .. 20) of INTEGER;
TABLE : array(1 .. 5) of LIST;
TABLE2 : array(1 .. 5,1 .. 20) of INTEGER;
```

No slice operations can be performed on TABLE2. Because the components of TABLE are single-dimension arrays, however, we can perform slice operations on those components. Here are some assignments that can be made to the components of TABLE:

```
TABLE(1)(15 .. 20) := (0,0,0,0,0,0);
TABLE(3)(5 .. 10) := TABLE(4)(5 .. 10);
TABLE(5)(1 .. 16) := TABLE(5)(2 .. 17);
TABLE(J)(A+1 .. B*2) := TABLE(J-1)(A+1 .. B*2);
TABLE(J/2)(SLICE) := TABLE(J)(SLICE);
TABLE(1 .. 2) := TABLE(3 .. 4);
```

The fourth and fifth assignments above illustrate two additional forms in which slices can be written. The fourth assignment shows a slice whose bounds are specified by expressions. Either or both bounds of a slice can be an expression, as long as the result of the expression conforms to the index constraint of the array. The fifth assignment shows a slice specified by a subtype identifier. Assuming that SLICE is a subtype of the index type, the range of SLICE indicates the bounds of the slice in the assignment.

5.4 STRING VARIABLES

A string variable is an array whose components are characters. A variable of this kind can be used to store and retrieve character strings. String variables enable us to manipulate textual information as we do numeric information. Ada provides the data type CHARACTER to serve as the component type of string variables. CHARACTER is an enumeration type whose elements are the 128 characters of the ASCII character set.

Literals of type CHARACTER consist of a single character enclosed by apostrophes. If the variable CHAR has been declared to have the type CHARACTER, then these assignments are valid:

```
CHAR := 'W';
CHAR := '?';
CHAR := '7';
CHAR := ' ';
CHAR := '';     --null
CHAR := ''';    --apostrophe
```

Some distinctions should be noted here. First, the character literal '7' is not interchangeable with the integer literal 7 or the string literal "7"; the three are associated with altogether different data types. Second, the space character (which appears in the fourth assignment) should not be confused with the null character. The space character is a printing character, while the null character is not.

Since CHARACTER is a discrete type, variables of type CHARACTER can be used to control *case* structures and *for* loops. No additional instantiation is needed for input and output of CHARACTER values. The following *for* loop prints all the characters between 'A' and 'Z':

```
for CHAR in 'A'..'Z' loop
    PUT(CHAR);
end loop;
```

Within the loop, CHAR takes the successive values 'A', 'B', 'C', and so on. Boolean comparisons can be made between CHARACTER values; the comparison operator symbols are defined as they are for numeric types and arrays. The relational order of CHARACTER values is defined to coincide with the character codes of the ASCII character set. These character codes are listed in appendix B. Usefully, the following relations hold:

```
'A' < 'B' < 'C' < ... < 'X' < 'Y' < 'Z'
'a' < 'b' < 'c' < ... < 'x' < 'y' < 'z'
'0' < '1' < '2' < ... < '7' < '8' < '9'
```

The discrete type attributes described in section 3.4 can be applied to CHARACTER. The attributes SUCC and PRED return the succeeding and preceding character in the character set. Here are some CHARACTER expressions in which these attributes appear:

```
CHARACTER'PRED('2')      --equals '1'
CHARACTER'SUCC('D')      --equals 'E'
CHARACTER'PRED('x')      --equals 'w'
CHARACTER'PRED(CHARACTER'SUCC('A'))      --equals 'A'
```

The attributes POS and VAL convert CHARACTER values into their integer character codes and vice versa. Since the character code for '0' is 48, we know that

```
CHARACTER'POS('0')      --equals 48
CHARACTER'VAL(48)       --equals '0'
CHARACTER'POS(CHARACTER'SUCC('0'))      --equals 49
```

To create a string variable, we merely declare a one-dimension array with the component type CHARACTER. If we want a string variable that can represent strings of twenty characters, we can write any of the following declarations:

```
SHORT_STR : array(1..20) of CHARACTER;
SHORT_STR2 : array(-5..14) of CHARACTER;
SHORT_STR3 : array(0..19) of CHARACTER;
```

These variables can now be assigned string values, as below:

```
SHORT__STR := "01234567890123456789";
SHORT__STR2 := "This is a string.  ";
SHORT__STR3 := "!@$#$% ^ : &*()__+ - = ][?>";
```

In each assignment, the value assigned to the variable is exactly twenty characters in length. As the assignments above show, character strings can serve as positional aggregates for string variables. The first assignment, for instance, will leave SHORT__STR(1) equal to '0', SHORT__STR(2) equal to '1', SHORT__STR(3) equal to '2', and so on.

Name aggregates can also be used to give a value to a string variable. The usage of name aggregates with strings follows the format of name aggregates for other array types. Here are some assignments in which name aggregates appear:

```
SHORT__STR := (1..20 => ' ');      --all blanks
SHORT__STR := (others => ' ');     --all blanks
SHORT__STR := (3 => '*', others => '-');
```

To simplify string declarations, Ada provides an array type called STRING, which can be regarded as having the following "invisible" declaration:

```
type STRING is array(NATURAL range <>) of CHARACTER;
```

Here are some constant and variable declarations in which the type STRING is used:

```
LINE : STRING(1..80);
TITLE : STRING(11..20) := "President ";
ALPHABET : constant STRING:= "ABCDEFGHIJKLMNOPQRSTUVWXYZ";
WARNING : STRING := "Ten seconds have elapsed.";
```

In the first two declarations, the index constraint is given explicitly. LINE is a string variable of length 80, while TITLE is a string variable of length 10. In the last two declarations, however, the index constraints are omitted. They are therefore derived from the lengths of the initial values. Since the declaration for ALPHABET specifies an initial value with twenty-six characters, ALPHABET is given the index constraint 1 . . 26. A similar derivation is made for the index constraint of WARNING.

Like other one-dimensional arrays, two strings can be compared with one another using the boolean comparison operators. The relational ordering of string variables follows the rules employed in general array comparisons, detailed in section 5.1. As noted earlier, these rules produce results that are generally consistent with the ordering of words in a dictionary. The leftmost characters are compared first; if they are equal, the comparison advances to the next character, and so on. So these boolean expressions are all true:

```
"Ada" = "Ada"
"Jenner" > "Fleming"
"Malthus" < "Marx"
"Brahe" <= "Brahms"
"Euler" >= "Euclid"
"Fourier" /= "Harvey"
```

A comparison can produce unexpected results if the two strings mix upper and lower case letters. As appendix B shows, lower case letters are greater than upper case letters. This means that the string "ada" is greater than "Ada", which in turn is greater than "ADA".

Ada provides two attributes for conversion between strings and values of discrete types. The attribute IMAGE accepts an expression and returns its string representation. The length of the string is determined by the number of characters needed to represent the value. Numeric values are preceded by either a minus sign or a space. Floating point values are returned in exponential form with a three-digit exponent; all other numeric values are returned in conventional form. Here are some attribute inquiries that use IMAGE:

```
INTEGER'IMAGE(300)            --equals " 300"
WEIGHT'IMAGE(-20)             --equals "-20"
FLOAT'IMAGE(+12.5)            --equals "1.25E+001"
MY__FIXED'IMAGE(25/2)         --equals "12.5"
DAYS'IMAGE(Monday)            --equals "MONDAY"
DAYS'IMAGE(DAYS'LAST)         --equals "SATURDAY"
INTEGER'IMAGE(ABS(X-Y))
FLOAT'IMAGE(DIST**2)
```

The attribute VALUE performs the inverse operation: it accepts a string (or a string expression) and converts it to a discrete type. An error condition occurs if the string does not contain a legal value of the type. Here are some inquiries that include this attribute:

```
INTEGER'VALUE("300")              --equals 300
FLOAT'VALUE("140.0")              --equals 1.4e+2
MY__FIXED'VALUE("3.14")           --equals 3.14
DAYS'VALUE("tuesday")             --equals TUESDAY
INTEGER'VALUE("10.0")             --error
INTEGER'VALUE("XYZ")              --error
POSITIVE'VALUE("-3")              --error
FLOAT'VALUE(FLOAT'IMAGE(X))       --equals X
```

Variants of GET and PUT are provided to simplify conversion between string types and scalar types. Instead of reading and printing values at the default file, they "read" and "print" using strings. Here is a GET statement that takes a fixed point value from a string and places it in a variable named FIXED__VAR:

```
GET("5.02", FIXED__VAR, LAST__POS);
```

The third item in the list, LAST__POS, is of type POSITIVE. After the GET is completed, the variable in this position will contain the index of the last character read. If the string does not contain a legal value, an error condition results. Here is a PUT statement that performs the converse operation:

```
PUT(STR__VAR,5.02,AFT=>3,EXP,=>0);
```

As described in section 4.4, AFT and EXP control the output format of real numbers. FORE cannot be included in this version of PUT; instead, FORE is automatically adjusted so that the string is filled. If STR__VAR is of type STRING(1 . . 6), the statement above will give it the value " 5.020". For integer conversions, only BASE can be supplied. WIDTH is adjusted to the length of the string.

An operator for performing catenation is available. To catenate a pair of strings is to combine them so they form a single string. Catenating the string "ABC" and the string "XYZ", for example, yields the string "ABCXYZ". The catenation operator is the ampersand ("&"). Catenation can actually be performed on any one-dimensional array type, though it is ordinarily a string operation. Here are some string expressions involving catenation:

```
"123" & "45"      --equals "12345"
LINE & "   "
WORD1 & "," & WORD2
```

The catenation operator can also be given one operand with an array type and one operand with the component type of the array. The result is an array that combines the two. If CHAR is a variable of type CHARACTER, we can write

```
"The value of CHAR is " & CHAR
```

When we assign a catenated array to an array variable, we must be careful to see that the lengths of both arrays match. If LINE is of type STRING(1 . . 10), for example, we cannot write any of these assignments:

```
LINE := LINE & "   ";
LINE := "ABCDE" & "FGH" & "IJK";
LINE := "!";
```

In each of these cases, an adjustment must be made so that the result of the string expression has exactly ten characters. We can circumvent this restriction somewhat by using slices. Here is an assignment that places a value in a string slice:

```
LINE(1..5) := "ABCDE";
```

If ABBREV is of type STRING(1 . . 5), then we can write assignments like these:

```
LINE(1..5):= ABBREV;
LINE(6..10):= ABBREV;
LINE(1..10):= ABBREV & ABBREV;
ABBREV:= LINE(16#6#..16#A#);
LINE(1..3):= LINE(3..5);      --overlapping is allowed
LINE(1..ABBREV'LENGTH):= ABBREV;
```

The final assignment in the series uses the array attribute LENGTH to determine the number of characters in ABBREV. Although this form is longwinded, it has a compensating advantage: it does not require that information about the declaration of ABBREV be present in the assignment. If the program is later modified so that ABBREV has a different length, the assignment will need no changes.

Importantly, an assignment to a string slice leaves the other components of the string unaffected. For this reason, it is good practice to "blank out" an array before a slice assignment. (Name aggregates are useful for this purpose.) For instance,

```
ABBREV(1..2):= "XX";
```

would not affect ABBREV(3 . . 5). If ABBREV had an initial value of "Plato", then this assignment would leave it with the value "XXato". The sequence below, on the other hand, averts unpredictable results of this kind:

```
ABBREV:= (others => ' ');  --all blanks
ABBREV(1..2):= "XX";
```

Many characters in the ASCII character set actually have no typographical representation. These characters are called *control characters* because they are often used to control the operation of external devices. Since these characters cannot appear in an Ada program, they must be referenced by the names that Ada provides for them. These names are listed in Appendix B. The character associated with character code 1, for instance, can be referenced as ASCII.SOH.

To write a character string that includes a control character, we must use catenation, name aggregates, or a similar device:

```
ABBREV:= "abc" & ASCII.SOH & "d";
ABBREV:= (1..ABBREV'LENGTH => ASCII.SOH);
```

The program in example 5.2 shows input–output of string variables. Notice that no additional instantiation is needed for string input–output. In this program, each component of the input string is tested for membership in VOWELS, an enumeration type. If the test succeeds, then the vowel count is incremented.

Example 5.2

```
with TEXT_IO; use TEXT_IO;
procedure VOWEL_COUNT is
```

```
    NUM : INTEGER := 0 ;
    LENGTH : NATURAL ;
    LINE : STRING(1 .. 80) ;
    type VOWELS is ('A','E','I','O','U','a','e','i','o','u') ;
    package IO__FOR__INT is new INTEGER__IO(INTEGER) ;
    use IO__FOR__INT ;
begin
    PUT__LINE("This program counts the numbers of vowels in") ;
    PUT__LINE("a line of text.") ;
    NEW__LINE ;
    PUT__LINE("Please enter your line.") ;
    GET__LINE(LINE,LENGTH) ;
    for I in 1 .. LENGTH loop
        if LINE(I) in VOWELS then
            NUM := NUM + 1 ;
        end if ;
    end loop ;
    NEW__LINE ;
    PUT(NUM) ;
    PUT__LINE("vowels were found.") ;
end VOWEL__COUNT ;
```

The GET procedure is not used in this program. When used with strings, GET is somewhat inflexible: it reads exactly the number of characters corresponding to the length of the variable. If the input has fewer characters, then an error condition results. Ada provides another string input procedure called GET__LINE, which stops reading at the end of the line or the end of the variable, whichever comes first. Along with a string variable, GET__LINE takes a variable of type NATURAL. After a GET__LINE is finished, this variable contains the subscript of the last character read. Components past the indicated subscript are undefined. In example 5.2, LENGTH is used for this purpose.

6

RECORDS

6.1 INVARIANT RECORDS

Along with arrays, which allow us to represent homogeneous collections of data, Ada provides another composite type: the *record*. Records are similar to arrays in that they are both formed of individual components. While the components of an array must share a common type, however, components of a record can have disparate types. Here is a declaration for a record type:

```
type ADDRESS is
    record
        HOUSE : INTEGER ;
        STREET : STRING(1 .. 20) ;
        CITY : STRING(1 .. 20) ;
        STATE : STRING(1 .. 2) ;
        ZIP : INTEGER range 1e4 .. 1e5 ;
    end record ;
```

The identifiers listed inside the record declaration are used to name the components of the new record. The component named HOUSE is of type INTEGER, the component named STREET is of type STRING, and so on. Record component names are analogous in function to the indices of an array. To reference a record component, we write the name of the record object followed by the name of the component iteself. The two identifiers are separated with a period. If a variable named MY__PLACE has been given the type ADDRESS, then we can write assignments like

```
MY__PLACE.HOUSE := 10230 ;
MY__PLACE.STREET := "Maplestead Lane        " ;
MY__PLACE.CITY := "Nowheresville          " ;
MY__PLACE.STATE := "VA" ;
MY__PLACE.ZIP := 12345 ;
```

Components with the same type can be grouped in the type declaration, as shown here:

```
type ADDRESS is
    record
        HOUSE : INTEGER ;
        STREET, CITY : STRING(1 .. 20) ;
        STATE : STRING(1 .. 2) ;
        ZIP : INTEGER range 1e4 .. 1e5 ;
    end record ;
```

A record component can be given a default initial value in its type declaration, as well:

```
type ADDRESS is
    record
        HOUSE : INTEGER := 0 ;
        STREET,CITY : STRING(1 .. 20) := (others => ' ') ;
        STATE : STRING(1 .. 2) := "  " ;
        ZIP : INTEGER range 1e4 .. 1e5 ;
    end record ;
```

Record aggregates, like array aggregates, can be written in positional form or name form. Components in a positional aggregate are written in the order of their appearance in the type declaration. Here are some assignments made with record aggregates:

```
MY__PLACE := (10230, "Maplestead Lane         ",
              "Nowheresville         ", "Va", 12345) ;    --positional
MY__PLACE := (HOUSE => 10230,
              STREET => "Maplestead Lane         ",
              CITY => "Nowheresville         ",
              STATE => "Va",ZIP => 12345 ;              --name
MY__PLACE := (HOUSE | ZIP => 0, STATE => "Va",
              CITY | STREET => (1 .. 20 => '?');        --name
MY__PLACE := (HOUSE | ZIP => 0, STATE => "Va",
              others => (1 .. 20 => '?') ;              --name
```

Like an array, a record can be manipulated in many situations as a single unit. Two record variables of the same type can be mixed in assignments and comparisons. (Only the equality and inequality operators are available for record comparisons; other relational tests, such as "greater than" or "less than," are not defined.) If HOME and OFFICE are variables of type ADDRESS, then statements like these are legal:

```
HOME := OFFICE ;
if HOME /= OFFICE then ...
if (HOME = OFFICE) and (HOME.ZIP > 23000) then ...
```

The components of a record can be of any type. Here is a declaration for a record type in which another record type is embedded:

```
type EMPLOYEE is
      record
            FIRST__NAME,LAST__NAME : STRING(1..20);
            RESIDENCE : ADDRESS;
            PHONE : STRING(1..10);
            PAY__SCALE : CHARACTER range 'A'..'Z';
      end record;
```

How do we reference a component of the embedded record? How, for instance, can we print an employee's house number? Since this component is located inside two nested records, we must provide both its own name and that of the record surrounding it. If FOREMAN is a variable of type EMPLOYEE, we can write

```
PUT(FOREMAN.RESIDENCE.HOUSE);
```

Similarly, here is an assignment that places a new value in the first three characters of the CITY component:

```
FOREMAN.RESIDENCE.CITY(1..3) := "St.";
```

Here is an *if* statement that examines the first character of the street name:

```
if FOREMAN.RESIDENCE.STREET(1) in 'N'..'Z' then...
```

Records are often used to encapsulate data that would otherwise be stored in "parallel" arrays. In this way, records help to keep logically related information together so it can be moved and accessed all at once. For instance, suppose we had a list of addresses. If we did not use records, we would need a sequence of declarations like this one:

```
HOUSE__NUMS : array(1..NAMES) of INTEGER;
STREETS : array(1..NAMES) of STRING(1..20);
CITIES : array(1..NAMES) of STRING(1..20);
STATES : array(1..NAMES) of STRING(1..2);
ZIP__CODES : array(1..NAMES) of INTEGER;
```

Under this arrangement, the information we have about a given person's address is scattered in five different places. Since an array can have any component type, however, we can construct an array whose components are records. Here is a declaration for such an array:

```
MAILING__LIST : array(1..NAMES) of ADDRESS;
```

To reference a single component of a single record of an array, we must specify the name of the array variable, the index of the desired record, and the name of the desired component. This statement will print component ZIP of MAILING__LIST(2):

```
PUT(MAILING__LIST(2).ZIP);
```

Assuming that NEW__ADDR is of type ADDRESS, this assignment will update an entry of MAILING__LIST:

```
MAILING__LIST(K) := NEW__ADDR;
```

Writing a long sequence of subscripts and component names can be error-prone and repetitious. Since a component that is buried inside a record may have to be referenced many times, Ada provides a facility for abbreviating these references. To make an abbreviation of this kind, we write a *renaming* declaration:

```
HOME : ADDRESS renames FOREMAN.RESIDENCE ;
```

The identifier HOME now refers to the same variable as FOREMAN.RESIDENCE. A renaming declaration for a variable (or a constant) must include three specifications. First, it must include the name of the object that is being renamed. In this case, the name is FOREMAN.RESIDENCE. The name that is given can be formed of component names, subscripts, and slices. Second, a renaming declaration must give the identifier for the type of the object. In this case, we know FOREMAN.RESIDENCE is of type ADDRESS. Finally, a renaming declaration must include the identifier that will be associated with the object. In this case, of course, the identifier is HOME.

A renaming declaration does not cause the previous name of the entity to be discarded. Thus, we can still write FOREMAN.RESIDENCE after it has been renamed. Here are some more declarations that rename variables and constants:

```
FIRST__DIGIT : CHARACTER renames PAYROLL.FICA(YTD)(1) ;
INITIAL : CHARACTER renames FOREMAN.LAST__NAME(1) ;
```

If the renamed entity is a constant, then the new name is treated as a constant as well. A renamed entity is subject to the same constraints whether it is referenced by its original name or its new one. Note that *goto* labels and loop identifiers cannot be renamed.

6.2 SIZE-VARIANT RECORDS

The record types that we examined in section 6.1 were all "invariant" in the sense that their structures could not be changed during program execution. If we know in advance that our data will take only one form, then an invariant record will meet our needs. In many instances, however, we will want to have a record whose structure can vary, chameleon-like, to accommodate different forms of data.

Ada provides *variant records* to allow for this possibility. In this section, we discuss records whose components can vary in size during execution; in the following section, we discuss records whose components can vary in type during execution. Both kinds of variants are predicated on the values in the *discriminants* of the record. A discriminant is a record component whose value indicates the form that the record should take. Here is a type declaration in which a discriminant appears:

```
type STACK(DEPTH : INTEGER range 0 .. MAX__SIZE := 4) is
    record
        OBJECTS : array(1 .. DEPTH) of FLOAT ;
    end record ;
```

The record type STACK is size-variant because the value of DEPTH determines the bounds of OBJECTS. (DEPTH is initially equal to 4.) A discriminant can appear in a component declaration only under restrictive conditions. First, it must be used as an array bound; it cannot be used elsewhere. Second, it must stand by itself; it cannot be part of an expression. The following type declaration is invalid on both counts:

```
type BAD(I : INTEGER range 0 .. 50 := 50) is
    record
        X : INTEGER range -1 .. I;            --not an array bound
        Y : array(0 .. I/2) of BOOLEAN;       --not alone
    end record ;
```

A record may have more than one discriminant. Here is a record with two:

```
type DYNAMIC__MATRIX(AXIS1 : INTEGER := 5; AXIS2 : DAYS := MONDAY) is
    record
        CHART : array(1 .. AXIS1,DAYS'FIRST .. AXIS2) of BOOLEAN ;
        X__PRECISION,Y__PRECISION : MY__FIXED ;
    end record ;
```

Here is a record in which the discriminant determines the bounds of an array subtype:

```
type VARYING__STRING(LENGTH : NATURAL := 80) is
    record
        LINE : STRING(1 .. LENGTH) ;
    end record ;
```

Assignments that modify only the discriminants of a record are not allowed. Discriminants cannot be updated except by an assignment to the entire record. The purpose of this restriction is to help maintain consistency between the value of the discriminant and the structure of the record. If WAITING is of type STACK, then the following assignment is illegal:

```
WAITING.DEPTH := 5 ;
```

These assignments are legal, however:

```
WAITING.OBJECTS := (1.0,2.0,3.0,4.0) ;        --assuming DEPTH is 4
WAITING := (5, (1.0,2.0,3.0,4.0,5.0)) ;       --now DEPTH is 5
```

If we want to define a record variable whose discriminants have fixed values, we can declare its discriminants to be *constrained*. To constrain the discriminants of a record, we supply the discriminant values in the variable declaration. The values can be supplied in positional notation or named notation. Here are some declarations for constrained record variables:

```
BUFFER : VARYING__STRING(16) ;
BUFFER : VARYING__STRING(LENGTH => 16) ;
DOT__GRID : DYNAMIC__MATRIX(5,TUESDAY) ;
DOT__GRID : DYNAMIC__MATRIX(AXIS1 => 5, AXIS2 => TUESDAY) ;
```

The values that are supplied for the discriminant are called *discriminant constraints*. Like a range constraint or an index constraint, a discriminant constraint can be incorporated into a subtype declaration as well as a variable declaration. Variables associated with a subtype that incorporates a discriminant constraint will, of course, have constrained discriminants. Here are some subtype declarations in which a discriminant constraint is included:

```
subtype EVENT__STACK is STACK(5) ;
subtype EVENT__STACK is STACK(DEPTH => 5) ;
```

Because its discriminants are constrained, a variable of type EVENT__STACK cannot be given a new discriminant value. An attempt to assign such a variable an array value with more than or less than five components would be invalid. If a record type specifies no default value for its discriminants, then variables of that type *must* be constrained. The following sequence of declarations is therefore illegal:

```
type BYTES(NUMBER : INTEGER) is
    record
        MAP : array(1 .. NUMBER) of CHARACTER ;
        IN__USE : array(1 .. NUMBER) of BOOLEAN ;
        LRU__COUNT : INTEGER ;
    end record ;
SWAP__AREA : BYTES ;        --error : SWAP__AREA must be constrained
```

A record type cannot be partially constrained and partially unconstrained; if one discriminant of a record is constrained, then all of its discriminants must be constrained. Ada provides an attribute named CONSTRAINED that allows a program to determine whether a record has constrained discriminants. CONSTRAINED accepts the name of a variable or constant that has discriminants. It returns a boolean TRUE if the entity is constrained; otherwise, it returns FALSE. If E is a variable of type EVENT__STACK, then the following *if* statement will cause a message to be printed:

```
if E'CONSTRAINED then
    PUT__LINE("The size of E cannot be changed.") ;
end if ;
```

The rules governing discriminant constraints can be summarized this way: if a record type provides default initial values for all of its discriminants, then a discriminant constraint is optional for variables of that type; if the default values are omitted, however, then discriminant constraints must be included. Additionally, the two modes cannot be mixed: a record is either constrained or unconstrained. If a record variable is constrained, then its size is invariant. If a record variable is unconstrained, on the other hand, then its size can be modified by assignments to the entire record.

6.3 TYPE-VARIANT RECORDS

A discriminant can be used to specify the structure that a record should take. Ada allows a record declaration to include a *variant part* for this purpose. The variant part of a record is similar in form to a *case* statement; each "branch" of the variant part corresponds to a set of possible discriminant values. Here is an example of a record with a variant part:

```
type ENTRY_TYPE is (BOOK,ARTICLE);
type BIBLIO(TAG : ENTRY_TYPE := ARTICLE) is
    record
        AUTHOR,TITLE : STRING(1..25);
        YEAR : INTEGER range 1000..9999;
        case TAG is
            when BOOK =>
                PUBLISHER,CITY : STRING(1..20);
            when ARTICLE =>
                JOURNAL : STRING(1..25);
                VOLUME,ISSUE : INTEGER;
        end case;
    end record;
```

AUTHOR, TITLE, and YEAR fall into the fixed part of the record; they have the same type regardless of the discriminant value. The remaining components are declared in the variant part; hence, their presence in the record depends on the value of TAG. When the discriminant TAG equals BOOK, the following components are available:

```
AUTHOR
TITLE
YEAR
PUBLISHER
CITY
```

When TAG equals ARTICLE, on the other hand, these are the components that can be referenced:

```
AUTHOR
TITLE
```

```
YEAR
JOURNAL
VOLUME
ISSUE
```

The default initial value for records of type BIBLIO is ARTICLE. To determine the current status of a record with a variant part, we need only examine its discriminant. Though the discriminant used with a variant part can have any discrete type, enumeration types are usually preferable for reasons of clarity. No more than one variant part can appear in a record declaration. If a variant part is included, it must follow all of the fixed part.

Suppose we have a variable of type BIBLIO named ENTRY. The program fragment below will start by printing the fixed part of ENTRY. It then examines the discriminant to see whether ENTRY contains a book or an article. If ENTRY contains a book, then the name of the publisher is printed. If ENTRY contains an article, on the other hand, then the name of the journal is printed.

```
PUT_LINE(ENTRY.AUTHOR);
PUT_LINE(ENTRY.TITLE);
PUT(ENTRY.YEAR);
NEW_LINE;
if ENTRY.TAG = BOOK then
    PUT_LINE (ENTRY.PUBLISHER);
else
    PUT_LINE(ENTRY.JOURNAL);
end if;
```

Several additional options should be noted. First, as with an ordinary *case* statement, a variant part can include an *others* clause. The variant associated with *others* is chosen when the discriminant has a value that is not listed elsewhere in the variant part. Second, more than one discriminant value can be associated with a single variant. Finally, a variant can consist simply of the reserved word *null;* Ada allows this construct so we can indicate that a particular variant does not contain any components. Here is a type declaration in which these options are used:

```
type ASSEMBLY_STAFF(TODAY : DAYS) is
    record
        FOREMAN : EMPLOYEE_ID;
        WELDER1,WELDER2 : EMPLOYEE_ID;
        case TODAY is
            when TUESDAY..THURSDAY =>
                PAINTER1,PAINTER2 : EMPLOYEE_ID;
            when MONDAY | FRIDAY =>
                MACHINIST1,MACHINIST2 : EMPLOYEE_ID;
            when others => null;       --weekend
        end case;
    end record;
```

Discriminants used with variant parts have the same properties as those used with varying-length arrays. In fact, a single discriminant could be used for both purposes. Here is a declaration for a subtype of BIBLIO in which TAG is constrained:

```
subtype BOOK__REF is BIBLIO(BOOK);
```

Here are some declarations that reference the type BIBLIO:

```
FOOTNOTES : array(1..100) of BIBLIO;
CITATION : BIBLIO(BOOK);
SUGGESTED : BIBLIO(TAG => ARTICLE);
```

CITATION and SUGGESTED are both constrained; hence, their structures cannot vary. Notice that records of type ASSEMBLY__STAFF must be constrained. Here is a declaration for a variable of type ASSEMBLY__STAFF:

```
CREW : ASSEMBLY__STAFF(MONDAY);
```

A constant of type ASSEMBLY__STAFF would be declared as

```
STD__MONDAY__CREW : constant ASSEMBLY__STAFF(MONDAY) := (...);
```

Here is a declaration for a type derived from ASSEMBLY__STAFF:

```
type FIRST__DAY is new ASSEMBLY__STAFF(TODAY => MONDAY);
```

As discussed in the previous section, Ada does not allow a discriminant of a record to be modified except during a complete record assignment. This rule protects us from a number of hazards, not the least of which is the possibility of a record becoming inconsistent with its discriminants. Hence, we can be confident that a record with a certain discriminant value does, in fact, have the indicated structure.

7

SUBPROGRAMS

7.1 FUNCTION SUBPROGRAMS

No language can offer every feature that a programmer might want, and Ada is no different. Ada allows us to overcome its omissions, however, by allowing us to declare our own subprograms. A subprogram is declared much like a program in miniature. Subprograms fall into two classes: *functions* and *procedures*. In this section, we discuss function declarations; in the next section, we turn to procedure declarations.

The difference between functions and procedures is that functions always return a result. One function that we might declare is an integer square root function. We will call the function SQRT. It will accept a value of type INTEGER and return a value of type INTEGER. A declaration for this function is shown in example 7.1.

Example 7.1

```
function SQRT(I : INTEGER) return INTEGER is
    INTERMEDIATE : FLOAT ;
    --This function computes the square root of an
    --integer by converting it to a floating point
    --value and then raising it to the power of ½.
    --The result is converted back to an integer.
begin
    INTERMEDIATE := FLOAT(I);
    INTERMEDIATE := INTERMEDIATE ** 0.5 ;
    return INTEGER(INTERMEDIATE) ;
end SQRT ;
```

Once declared, SQRT can be used in integer expressions. Here are some statements in which SQRT is called:

```
    LENGTH__OF__EDGE := SQRT(AREA) ;
    PUT(SQRT(2**8)) ;
```

```
if HYPOTENUSE /= SQRT(A**2 + B**2) then
    PUT__LINE("This is not a right triangle.");
end if;
```

The values that are passed to a subprogram are its *actual parameters*. When a call is made, the actual parameters supplied by the program are associated with the corresponding *formal parameters* of the subprogram. Since SQRT has a formal parameter of type INTEGER, an integer value must be passed. This value is then available to the subprogram, which can use I as an integer constant.

The first line of the declaration is the *subprogram specification*. It supplies the name of the function, the types of its parameters, and the type of value it returns. The formal parameters are listed in the parentheses following the function name. A subprogram can have any number of parameters; the list is written as a sequence of variable declarations. The parameter list is omitted if the subprogram takes no parameters. Here are some specifications for other function subprograms:

```
function DAYS__IN__MONTH(THIS__MONTH: MONTHS) return
    INTEGER range 1..31;
function RANDOMIZE return FLOAT;
function FIND__STRING(LINE, SUBSTR : VARYING__STRING) return
    BOOLEAN;
function SCALAR__MULT(C : INTEGER; X : MATRIX) return MATRIX;
```

Parameter types must be given as type identifiers. In the calling program, parameters can be written in positional notation or name notation. For instance,

```
DAYS__IN__MONTH(JUNE)                          --positional
DAYS__IN__MONTHS(THIS__MONTH => JUNE)          --named
```

The specification can provide default values for its parameters. If a parameter has a default value, then it can be omitted when the subprogram is called. Defaults can be given as expressions; in that case, they are evaluated at the time of the call. Here is a specification that provides a default value:

```
function ANALOG__TO__DIGITAL(CHANNEL : NATURAL := 0) return
    SHORT__INT;
```

If *all* of the parameters are omitted from a function call, then the function name is written alone. The same form is used to call a function that has no parameters. Thus, we write

```
R := RANDOMIZE;
```

Since the default for the CHANNEL parameter of ANALOG__TO__DIGITAL is 0, each of these function calls has the same effect :

```
SAMPLE := ANALOG__TO__DIGITAL;
SAMPLE := ANALOG__TO__DIGITAL(0);
SAMPLE := ANALOG__TO__DIGITAL(CHANNEL => 0);
```

Following the specification, the next part of a subprogram is its *declarative part*. Identifiers that are declared inside a subprogram are said to be *local* to the subprogram. The function shown in example 7.1 has a local variable named INTERMEDIATE. An entity associated with a local identifier is available only inside the subprogram; other parts of the program cannot refer to it. For instance, INTERMEDIATE is not defined outside SQRT. Each time SQRT is called, INTERMEDIATE is initially undefined. After SQRT is completed, INTERMEDIATE ceases to exist until the next call.

The last part of a subprogram declaration is the *body*. Like the body of a program, the body of a subprogram specifies the steps to be followed when it is executed. Any Ada statements can appear in a subprogram body. An additional statement, the *return* statement, is also available inside subprograms. When a *return* is encountered, the subprogram is terminated. The calling program then resumes at the point following the call.

In a function, a *return* also indicates the value that will be returned. This value must have the result type given in the specification. As we have seen, SQRT returns a value of type INTEGER. If no *return* is reached in a function, then its result is undefined; in this case, of course, an error condition is likely to follow. Here are some examples of *return*s that can appear in function declarations:

```
return ABS(Y/X);
return 2 ** (BITS + 1);
return STR1 & " " & STR2;
```

The function shown in example 7.2 calculates the average of the components of an array. The average is returned as a floating point number. Both the component type and the index type of LIST are assumed to be subtypes of INTEGER. Since attribute inquiries are used to determine the range of the index, LIST can have any number of components.

Example 7.2

```
function MEAN(NUMBERS : LIST) return FLOAT is
    SUM : FLOAT := 0.0;
    --This function accepts a one-dimension array
    --with integer components and returns their
    --average.
begin
    for COUNT in LIST'RANGE loop
        SUM := SUM + NUMBERS(COUNT);
    end loop;
    return SUM/FLOAT(LIST'LENGTH);
end MEAN;
```

A subprogram that calls itself is said to be *recursive*. Some problems are most naturally expressed in a recursive form. One problem of this kind is the factorial function. Defined without recursion, the factorial of *X* (written *X!*) equals X*(X − 1)*(X − 2)* . . . *3*2*1. In recursive form, X! can be defined as

```
X * (X - 1)!     --if X > 1
1                --if X = 1
```

The program shown in example 7.3 uses this definition. It calls a recursive function named FACTORIAL, which in turn calls itself until the terminating case is reached. Execution then "backtracks" as each function call returns a value to the level above it.

Example 7.3

```
with TEXT_IO; use TEXT_IO;
procedure GET_FACTORIAL is
    VALUE : POSITIVE;
    package POS_IO is new INTEGER_IO(POSITIVE);
    use POS_IO;
    --function declaration starts here
    function FAC(X : POSITIVE) return POSITIVE is
        begin
            if X = 1 then
                return 1;
            else
                return X * FAC(X - 1);
            end if;
        end FAC;
begin     --main
    PUT_LINE("Enter the number for which a factorial is desired:");
    GET(VALUE);
    if VALUE < 1 then
        PUT_LINE("Only positive numbers have factorials.");
    else
        PUT(FAC(VALUE));
        NEW_LINE;
    end if;
end GET_FACTORIAL;
```

Each recursive call creates a distinct set of local variables. Hence, a recursive call does not affect the variables inside the calling function. Here is an example of a recursive calling sequence:

```
FAC(4)      = 4 * FAC(3)
            = 4 * 3 * FAC(2)
            = 4 * 3 * 2 * FAC(1)
            = 4 * 3 * 2 * 1
            = 24
```

7.2 PROCEDURE SUBPROGRAMS

Procedures in Ada are declared in much the same way as functions. Example 7.4 shows a declaration for a procedure named UNDERLINE. This procedure accepts a string parameter and prints it, underlining all of its nonblank characters.

STR__TYPE is assumed to be a type identifier declared elsewhere by the programmer.

Example 7.4

```
procedure UNDERLINE(LINE : STR__TYPE) is
    UL : constant CHARACTER := '__';
    SP : constant CHARACTER := ' ';
    --This procedure prints LINE and then prints
    --underlines beneath each nonblank character.
begin
    NEW__LINE ;
    PUT(LINE) ;
    NEW__LINE ;       --start at the beginning of the next line
    for POS in LINE'RANGE loop
        if LINE(POS) /=' ' then
            PUT(UL) ;     --write an underline
        else
            PUT(SP) ;     --write a space
        end if;
    end loop ;
end UNDERLINE ;
```

Assuming that STR__TYPE is of length 14, the following is a valid call to UNDERLINE:

```
UNDERLINE("A test string.") ;
```

As example 7.4 indicates, the *return* statement is optional in procedure subprograms. If no *return* is encountered, execution of a procedure terminates at its closing *end*. Since a procedure does not return a formal result, a *return* that appears in a procedure cannot give a value.

Though a procedure does not return a formal result, information can still be passed from a procedure back to its caller. Ada allows us to choose from several *parameter modes* for this purpose. The modes are called *in*, *out*, and *in out*. The *in* mode is the default for procedures and is the only allowable mode for functions. An *in* parameter acts as a constant; its value is provided by the caller and cannot be changed inside the subprogram.

An *out* parameter, on the other hand, can be used like a variable. When a subprogram is called, its *out* parameters are initially undefined. They receive their values inside the subprogram. When the subprogram terminates, the values of the *out* parameters are placed in the corresponding parameters of the caller. Finally, an *in out* parameter combines the features of both: its initial value is passed from the caller to the subprogram, and its final value is passed from the subprogram to the caller. Example 7.5 shows a procedure that uses an *in out* parameter.

Example 7.5

```
procedure COMPRESS(LINE : in out STR__TYPE) is
    --This procedure takes all the blanks from LINE.
    --The string is then padded with nulls on the right.
    POS : POSITIVE ;
```

```
begin
    POS := LINE'FIRST;
    while POS <= LINE'LAST loop
        if LINE(POS) = ' ' then
            LINE := LINE(LINE'FIRST..POS-1) & LINE(POS+1..LINE'LAST) & " ";
        else
            POS := POS + 1;
        end if;
    end loop;
end COMPRESS;
```

If a parameter mode is specified, it precedes the identifier that gives the data type. During a call to COMPRESS, the parameter corresponding to LINE would be modified to reflect the manipulations inside the procedure. If ID__CODE were a variable of type STR__TYPE, then the following statement would compress the contents of ID__CODE:

```
COMPRESS(ID__CODE);
```

An *out* or *in out* parameter must be given as a variable. Obviously, a procedure cannot transmit values through a constant or an expression. When COMPRESS terminates, for instance, there will be no place to put its results unless LINE is a variable. The following call is therefore invalid:

```
COMPRESS("A test string.");
```

Different parameter modes can appear in the same procedure specification. (As noted previously, *in* is the default if no mode is listed.) Here are more specifications in which parameter modes are given:

```
procedure SWAP(X,Y : in out FLOAT) is
procedure NUM__TO__STRING(I : INTEGER; S : out STR__TYPE) is
procedure MOVE__HEAD(X,Y : in INTEGER := 0) is
procedure PRINT__REF(CITATION : in BIBLIO) is
```

As with function calls, procedure calls can be made with named or positional parameters. If a procedure has no parameters, then only the procedure name is written. Here are some additional examples of procedure calls:

```
CLEAR__SCREEN;
UPDATE__RECORD(REC);
FIRE__PHASERS(ENERGY => 1000, TARGET => T1);
```

Formal parameters can be given unconstrained types in the subprogram specification. In that case, they are constrained with the constraints of the values they receive. Using unconstrained types this way makes a subprogram more flexible, because it can then handle arrays and records of different sizes. For instance, if the parameter type in example 7.5 were an unconstrained array type, such as STRING, then COMPRESS could take strings of any size. Since the body of COMPRESS relies on attribute enquiries to determine the bounds of the string, no additional changes would be necessary. Assuming that STR__TYPE is a constrained subtype of STRING, the present version of the subprogram requires strings with particular bounds.

7.3 SCOPE AND VISIBILITY

Subprogram declarations can be nested inside other subprograms. This is allowed in part for the sake of consistency and in part for the sake of modularity. It is consistent because it follows from the idea that a subprogram is a program in miniature. Just as the main program can include subprograms, so can the subprograms themselves. It promotes modularity because it allows a subprogram to be divided into parts that are smaller and less complex.

This flexibility introduces an additional difficulty, however. If we allow subprograms to be nested, then we must have rules for deciding where an entity (such as a variable, a constant, or a type) is defined. The rules Ada provides for this purpose are called its *scope* rules. The scope of an entity is simply the region where it can be referenced.

The most general case is an entity that appears in the declarative part of a program or subprogram. An object of this kind is available from the point of its declaration to the end of the program or subprogram. Hence, it can be referenced in the body of the program or subprogram and also in the bodies of any nested subprograms. Example 7.6 shows the scope of such an object. POINTER is a local variable of ACCEPT__COMMAND. It is available in the shaded region; its scope includes CONV__TO__UPPER, the body of ACCEPT__COMMAND, and part of the declarations in ACCEPT__COMMAND.

Example 7.6

```
procedure ACCEPT__COMMAND(LINE : out STR__TYPE) is
    CONSOLE : constant STRING(1 .. 5) := "TT01:";
    POINTER : POSITIVE;
    IN__CHAR : CHARACTER;
    function CONV__TO__UPPER(CH : CHARACTER) return CHARACTER is
    begin
        ...
    end CONV__TO__UPPER;
begin
    ...
    end ACCEPT__COMMAND;
```

The scope of a formal parameter of a subprogram follows the same pattern. A formal parameter is available from the point of its appearance to the end of the subprogram. Example 7.7 is shaded to show the scope of CH. (If CONV__TO__UPPER included nested subprograms of its own, CH would be available inside these subprograms as well.)

Example 7.7

```
Procedure ACCEPT__COMMAND(LINE : out STR__TYPE) is
    CONSOLE : constant STRING(1 .. 5) := "TT01:";
    POINTER : POSITIVE ;
    IN__CHAR : CHARACTER ;
    function CONV__TO__UPPER(CH : CHARACTER) return CHARACTER is
    begin
        ...
    end CONV__TO__UPPER ;
begin
    ...
end ACCEPT__COMMAND ;
```

The scope of a loop parameter is restricted to the loop itself. As we saw in section 2.4, loop parameters do not appear in a declarative part. They are declared implicitly by their use. Example 7.8 is shaded to show the scope of loop parameter J.

Example 7.8

```
procedure MAKE__TRANSITIVE(G : in out GRID) is
    --G is a square array of boolean components.
begin
    for I in G'RANGE(1) loop
        for J in G'RANGE(2) loop
            if G(I,J) then
              G(I,I) := TRUE ;
              G(J,J) := TRUE ;
            end if ;
        end loop ;
    end loop ;
end MAKE__TRANSITIVE ;
```

Statement labels for *goto* and loop names for *exit* are also declared implicitly. The scope of a label is effectively the body of the program or subprogram in which it appears. From this it follows that *goto*'s and *exit*'s cannot transfer control out of a subprogram or into a subprogram. Transfers made with these facilities must start and stop in the same body.

If a nested program gives an identifier another meaning, then we are left with a conflict to resolve. The subprograms shown in example 7.9 declare PORT twice. In the body of NEXT__BYTE, no ambiguity is present. The body of CLEAR __BUFFER, however, is within the scope of two entities named PORT. Both entities happen to be variables of the same type. Nonetheless, they are distinct.

Ada provides rules of *visibility* to govern these conflicts. Though a subprogram can be within the scope of multiple entities having the same name, only one of the entities can be visible. When an identifier is given different meanings in nested subprograms, the visible entity is the one in the nearest enclosing declaration. The others are said to be *hidden*. In CLEAR__BUFFER, the identifier PORT refers to the inner declaration, because its outer declaration is hidden from view.

Example 7.9

```
function NEXT__BYTE is
    PORT : INTEGER ;
    procedure CLEAR__BUFFER is
        PORT : INTEGER ;
    begin
        --PORT refers to the inner declaration here
        . . .
    end CLEAR__BUFFER ;
begin
    --PORT refers to the outer declaration here
    . . .
end NEXT__BYTE ;
```

To access a hidden entity, we qualify its name with the name of the subprogram in which it is declared. In the body of NEXT__BYTE, no qualification is needed, because only one PORT is defined. In CLEAR__BUFFER, we can access the outer PORT by writing

```
NEXT__BYTE.PORT
```

The inner PORT, which is visible, needs no qualification here. The assignment below sets the inner PORT equal to the outer PORT:

```
PORT := NEXT__BYTE.PORT ;
```

Repetitious use of qualifiers can be avoided with a renaming declaration. As we saw in section 6.1, lengthy sequences of identifiers can be given abbreviated names. Here is a renaming declaration that associates NEXT__BYTE.PORT with the identifier PORT2:

```
PORT2 : INTEGER renames NEXT__BYTE.PORT ;
```

We should note that referring to hidden identifiers is generally a poor practice. In fact, a well-constructed subprogram refers only to its parameters and its local variables. Otherwise, it becomes dependent on the internal details of the calling program or subprogram. If we write CLEAR__BUFFER so that it accesses NEXT__BYTE.PORT, we are requiring that a subprogram named NEXT__BYTE be present and that it have a variable named PORT. Subsequent changes to the program may leave this assumption incorrect. Keeping subprograms independent ensures that changes in one subprogram will not lead to unexpected errors in another.

7.4 SUBPROGRAM OVERLOADING

Just as identifiers for constants, variables, and types can be given multiple definitions, subprogram identifiers can be given multiple definitions as well. When the scope of one definition overlaps with the scope of another, an ambiguity results.

In most cases, ambiguous subprogram calls can be resolved by their context. Subprogram identifiers that fall in this category are overloaded. A subprogram identifier falls in this category if its declarations differ in the types, order, or names of their parameters. If an identifier refers to multiple functions, then their result types are also considered. (Other aspects of the parameters, such as their modes or default values, are not used to distinguish subprogram declarations.) A subprogram call is illegal if its meaning cannot be determined from any of these tests. The following specifications show an example of valid overloading:

```
function SINE(RADIANS : FLOAT) return FLOAT is
    begin
      ...
    end SINE ;
function SINE(DEGREES : INTEGER range 0 .. 360) return FLOAT is
    begin
      ...
    end SINE ;
```

Since expresssions of type FLOAT can always be distinguished from expressions of type INTEGER, there is no chance of an ambiguous call. If a call to SINE has a parameter of type FLOAT, then the subprogram corresponding to the first specification will be invoked. If the parameter is of type INTEGER, then the subprogram corresponding to the second specification will be used instead.

Some types share common literals, in which case an ambiguous call can be made. Say NAME and CITY are both twenty-character string types. The following specifications, then, open the possibility of an ambiguous call:

```
procedure UPDATE__SCREEN(N : NAME) is
procedure UPDATE__SCREEN(C : CITY) is
```

Since NAME and CITY have the same literals, a call like this one cannot be resolved:

```
UPDATE__SCREEN("Williamsburg        ");
```

Two kinds of disambiguation are available. First, the calls can be made in name notation, as below:

```
UPDATE__SCREEN(N => "Johnston            ");
UPDATE__SCREEN(C => "Williamsburg        ");
```

Alternately, the literals can be qualified, as discussed in section 3.1. Here are two calls that use this mechanism:

```
UPDATE__SCREEN(NAME'("Johnston            "));
UPDATE__SCREEN(CITY'("Williamsburg        "));
```

Of course, calls to UPDATE____SCREEN are not ambiguous in any case unless literals are passed. Expressions involving named objects (such as variables) have readily discernible types. If ROSTER is an array with components of type NAME, then this call needs no further qualification:

```
UPDATE__SCREEN(ROSTER(2));
```

We have seen that Ada's operator symbols are already overloaded. The symbol "*", for instance, is defined to take operands of any numeric type. These symbols can be overloaded further with subprogram declarations. Logical, relational, and arithmetic operators can be used to designate function subprograms, as in these specifications:

```
function "and"(S1,S2 : STATUS) return STATUS is
function "<"(FIRST,SECOND : BIBLIO) return BOOLEAN is
function "+"(C1,C2 : COMPLEX) return COMPLEX is
function "-"(A : ANGLE) return ANGLE is
```

The symbols "+" and "−" can be given either unary or binary declarations. The "not" and "abs" operators must be given unary declarations. All others must be binary. The first three specification lines above are examples of binary declarations. They take two parameters, which are passed as the left operand and the right operand of the operator. The fourth specification is unary.

Suppose the "<" operator has been defined for operands of type BIBLIO, as in the second specification above. That is, suppose we have written a function named "<" that takes two BIBLIO operands and returns a boolean result. If MY__LIB is an array with components of type BIBLIO, the "<" operator could be invoked to compare them:

```
if MY__LIB(1) < MY__LIB(2) then
    TEMP := MY__LIB(1);
    MY__LIB(1) := MY__LIB(2);
    MY__LIB(2) := TEMP;
end if;
```

If PATH is a variable of type ANGLE, this assignment will cause it to be negated, in whatever way the negation operator has been defined:

```
PATH := -PATH;
```

A number of restrictions apply to operator overloading. First, the membership operators *(in, not in)* and the short circuit control forms *(and then, or else)* cannot be overloaded. Second, the "=" and "/=" symbols cannot be redefined for any of the types we have used to this point. Third, functions designated by operator symbols cannot have default parameters. This last restriction follows from the fact that operands cannot be omitted when an operator is called: a binary operator always takes exactly two operands, and a unary operator always takes exactly one.

Overloading of operators is especially useful when we are manipulating derived types. While a subtype is not distinct from its base type, a derived type is considered distinct from its parent. Suppose we have the following declarations:

```
type PRICE is new INTEGER;
type UNITS is new INTEGER;
```

Values of type PRICE or UNITS cannot be mixed in expressions with values of type INTEGER unless an explicit conversion is made. The two derived types cannot be mixed with each other, either. If P is of type PRICE and U is of type UNITS, then expressions like P*U or P+U are not allowed by Ada's predefined operators. These expressions violate the rules of type compatibility set down for the operators.

Rigid checking of derived types offers a valuable benefit: it prevents us from writing illogical expressions. The expression P+U, for instance, has no meaning; adding prices and quantities cannot produce a useful result. Some mixed operations, however, do produce a useful result. Overloading allows us to define these operations. Example 7.10 shows a pair of function declarations that allows prices and quantities to be multiplied.

Example 7.10

```
function "*"(PR : PRICE; QTY : UNITS) return MY__FIXED is
begin
    return MY__FIXED(PR) * MY__FIXED(QTY);
end "*";

function "*"(QTY : UNITS; PR : PRICE) return MY__FIXED is
begin
    return MY__FIXED(QTY) * MY__FIXED(PR);
end "*";
```

The first declaration defines expressions like P*U, which now return a value of type MY__FIXED. The second declaration defines the commutative form U*P. Expressions of type PRICE and of type UNITS can now be multiplied. (If PRICE and UNITS were merely subtypes of INTEGER, on the other hand, then multiplication would be available as a predefined operation.)

8

ACCESS TYPES

8.1 SCALAR TYPE ALLOCATION

Most of the constants and variables in an Ada program can be specified in its declarative part. On some occasions, however, we may want to create them dynamically—that is, we may want to define additional objects during execution. For this purpose, Ada provides *access values*. An access value gives the location of another value. Here is a declaration for an access type:

```
type INT__PTR is access INTEGER;
```

A value of type INT__PTR can represent the location of an integer variable. The word *access* in the declaration indicates that INT__PTR is an access type. An access value is said to *designate* an object. If P is of type INT__PTR, then P can designate an integer variable. P can designate different variables at different times.

To create a variable for P to designate, we use an *allocator*. The reserved word *new* identifies an allocator. Here is an assignment that uses an allocator to give P a value:

```
P := new INTEGER;
```

We now have a new integer variable. To reference it, we follow P with the reserved word *all*. Here is an assignment that sets the new variable equal to 0:

```
P.all := 0;
```

Here is a statement that prints the new variable:

```
PUT(P.all);
```

If we want to discard this variable and create another, we simply execute another allocator. The allocator can also specify the initial value of the variable. For instance,

```
P := new INTEGER (3);      --P.all equals 3 initially
```

To illustrate some operations on access values, we will use the following declarations:

```
type AT__FLOAT is access FLOAT range 0.0 .. 2.0;
F1,F2 : AT__FLOAT;
```

The variables that F1 and F2 designate must meet the range constraint given in the declaration. Here are two assignments that cause F1 and F2 to designate different variables:

```
F1 := new FLOAT (1.0);
F2 := new FLOAT (1.0);
```

We can now make assignments to the designated variables:

```
F1.all := F1.all + 0.5;      --equals 1.5
F2.all := 0.85;
```

We can reverse the process by assigning an access variable the literal *null*. An access variable that equals *null* designates no object. (All access variables equal *null* initially.) This assignment will cause the variable designated by F2 to be lost:

```
F2 := null;
```

This assignment, on the other hand, will cause F2 to designate the same variable as F1:

```
F2 := F1;
```

From these examples, we can see that assignments to F2 and assignments to F2.all have very different effects. In the first case, we are modifying an access value; in the second, we are modifying the variable that it designates. In fact, F2 and F2.all have entirely different types: F2 is of type AT__FLOAT, while F2.all is of type FLOAT.

Assignments made to access variables must follow the usual requirements of type compatibility. Hence, an access variable cannot be assigned a value of a different access type. Since P is of type INT__PTR and F1 is of type AT__FLOAT, the following assignments are illegal:

```
F1 := P;
P := F1;
```

Unlike an access variable, an access constant cannot be assigned new access values during execution. Access constants can designate only one object. (The value of the designated object can be modified, however.) Here is a declaration for an access constant:

```
LOCATION : constant INT__PTR := new INTEGER (1);
```

Assignments like this one are valid:

```
LOCATION.all := 2 ** I;
```

Assignments to the access value itself, as below, are not permitted:

```
LOCATION := P;
```

The form shown above for initializing access constants can also be used with access variables. Here is a declaration sequence that defines an access variable and creates an object for it to designate:

```
type SECTOR is (STAR,STARBASE,STARSHIP,BAD__GUYS);
type SECTOR__PTR is access SECTOR;
OUR__SECTOR : SECTOR__PTR := new SECTOR;
```

This declaration gives the designated object an initial value as well:

```
OUR__SECTOR : SECTOR__PTR := new SECTOR (STARSHIP);
```

8.2 COMPOSITE TYPE ALLOCATION

When we use access values to designate objects with composite types, additional conveniences of notation are available to us. First of all, we can refer to individual components within the object. Suppose we have the following declarations:

```
type DATE is record
        DAY : INTEGER range 1 .. 31;
        MONTH : INTEGER range 1 .. 12;
        YEAR : INTEGER range 1 .. 9999;
    end record;
type REMINDER is record
        MESSAGE : STRING(1 .. 20);
        EVENT : DATE;
    end record;
type DATE__PTR is access DATE;
type REM__PTR is access REMINDER;
BIRTHDAYS : array(1 .. 50) of DATE__PTR;
MEMO : REM__PTR;
```

DATE and REMINDER are composite types. Using the notation presented in the previous section, we can refer to access variables that designate these types. For instance,

```
BIRTHDAYS(1)            --of type DATE__PTR
BIRTHDAYS(1).all        --of type DATE
MEMO                    --of type REM__PTR
MEMO.all                --of type REMINDER
```

To access individual components within the designated objects, we add the desired indices or component identifiers. In this case, the *all* suffix is optional. As a stylistic matter, though, keeping the *all* will help us remember that we are working with an access value. Here are some assignments that refer to components of the records:

```
BIRTHDAYS(I).all.YEAR := 1955;
BIRTHDAYS(J/2).all.MONTH := 3;
MEMO.all.EVENT := BIRTHDAYS.all(42);
MEMO.all.EVENT.MONTH := BIRTHDAYS.all(30).MONTH;
MEMO.all.MESSAGE := "Send thank-you note";
MEMO.all.MESSAGE := (1..20 => ' ');
MEMO.all.MESSAGE(1) := '*';
```

To create an object of type DATE or REMINDER, we can use a conventional allocator, as below:

```
MEMO := new REMINDER;
for COUNT in BIRTHDAYS'RANGE loop
    BIRTHDAYS(COUNT) := new DATE;
end loop;
```

The assignments below are each equivalent to the loop given above:

```
BIRTHDAYS := (1..50 => new DATE);
BIRTHDAYS := (BIRTHDAYS'RANGE => new DATE);
```

Conversely, we should note, this assignment causes the components of BIRTHDAYS to designate no object at all:

```
BIRTHDAYS := (1..50 => null);
```

As with scalar type allocation, initial values can be given to composite type objects when they are created. If an initial value is desired, it is provided as an aggregate within the allocator. Here are some assignments in which initial values are given:

```
BIRTHDAY(1) := new DATE (3,9,1961);     --positional
BIRTHDAY(1) := new DATE (DAY | MONTH => 1, YEAR => 1900);     --name
MEMO := new REMINDER ("Buy present for L.K.", (1,8,1984));
MEMO := new REMINDER (MESSAGE => MY__STR, EVENT => MY__DATE);
```

If the type of the object is an unconstrained array or record, then the allocator must either give an initial value or impose an explicit constraint. This requirement is consistent with those that apply to ordinary object declarations. Suppose we have the following unconstrained types:

```
type VISITS is array(INTEGER range <>) of REMINDER;
type LOGIN(CODED : BOOLEAN) is
        record
            USER : STRING(1 .. 6);
            case CODED is
                when TRUE => CODE : INTEGER;
                when FALSE => DAY : DATE;
            end case;
        end record;
type VISITS__PTR is access VISITS;
type LOGIN__PTR is access LOGIN;
```

As we saw in chapter 6, a variable of type VISITS must be given an initial value or an index constraint. The same is true when an object of type VISITS is created by an allocator. Say V is a VISITS__PTR variable. Of the following assignments, the first two are valid and the last is invalid:

```
V := new VISITS(1 .. 5 => (1,1,1900));     --initial value
V := new VISITS(1 .. 5);     --index constraint
V := new VISITS;     --neither (erroneous)
```

Likewise, we have seen that a variable of type LOGIN must be given an initial value or a discriminant constraint. If L is of type LOGIN__PTR, then the first and second allocators below meet this requirement, while the third does not:

```
L := new LOGIN (CODED => TRUE, USER => "ABX834", CODE => 3);
L := new LOGIN (FALSE);
L := new LOGIN;
```

The object designated by an access value can include components that designate other objects. Importantly, we can define composite types with components that designate other objects of the same type. As we will see in the next section, this capability is valuable because it allows us to form collections of objects that are "chained together." It also presents a dilemma of sorts. Which do we declare first: the composite type or the access type that designates it?

The answer lies in between. When a composite type has recursive components of this kind, it must be declared twice: once before the declaration of the access type and once afterward. In its first appearance, it is declared incompletely: only its name and discriminant part are given. In its second appearance, a full declaration is provided. Here is an example of such a sequence:

```
type LIST;
type LIST__PTR is access LIST;
type LIST is record
```

```
        DATA : INTEGER ;
        NEXT : LIST__PTR ;
    end record ;
```

Both declarations of LIST are necessary. If LIST were fully declared before LIST__PTR, then its reference to LIST__PTR could not be resolved. On the other hand, if LIST__PTR were declared first, then its reference to LIST could not be resolved. The incomplete declaration allows us to introduce LIST without referring to other identifiers.

8.3 STACKS

A stack is an arrangement of data with one entry point, called the *top*. An item can be added to the top of a stack or deleted from it. Hence, the last item to be added to a stack is always the first to come out. Adding an item to a stack is called a *push* operation; deleting an item is said to be a *pop* operation. As figure 8.1 shows, both operations take place at the top.

One way to represent a stack is to set aside an array variable for its contents and a scalar variable to point to the top. If we know that the stack will contain no more than 100 elements, this sequence of declarations will form the needed objects:

```
type DATA__PART is array(INTEGER range <>) of ITEM__TYPE ;
STK : DATA__PART(1 .. 100) ;
TOP : INTEGER range 0 .. 100 ;
```

Example 8.1 shows procedures that perform push and pop operations on STK. When the procedures are called, they start by checking TOP to see whether the given operation is valid. (Obviously, an item cannot be pushed onto a stack that is full or popped from an empty one.) Before the procedures terminate, they update

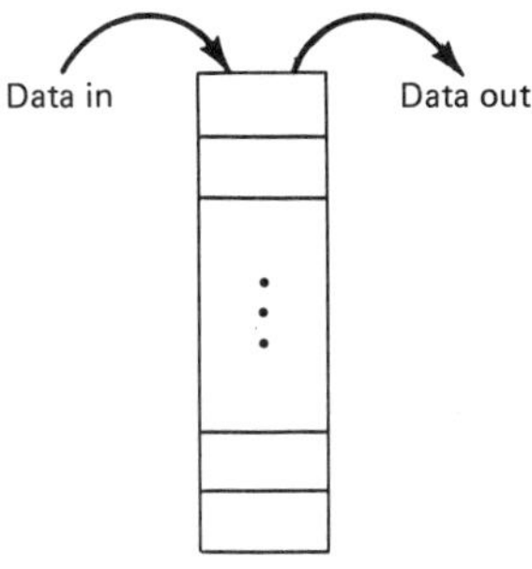

Figure 8.1: A stack

TOP to reflect the change. For instance, repeated calls to POP will eventually cause TOP to reach zero, at which point STK must be empty.

Example 8.1

```
procedure PUSH(I : ITEM__TYPE) is
begin
    if TOP = STK'LAST then
        PUT("Stack is full.");
    else
        TOP := TOP + 1;
        STK(TOP) := I;
    end if;
end PUSH;

procedure POP(out I : ITEM__TYPE) is
begin
    if TOP = 0 then
        PUT("Stack is empty.");
    else
        I := STK(TOP);
        TOP := TOP - 1;
    end if;
end POP;
```

Using unconstrained record types, we can encapsulate the data and the pointer of a stack into one variable. Here is a declaration that creates a unified stack type:

```
type STACK(TOP : INTEGER := 0) is
        record
            DATA : array(1 .. TOP) of ITEM__TYPE;
        end record;
```

Procedures PUSH and POP for this representation are shown in example 8.2. Rather than operating on a particular stack, as in example 8.1, these procedures accept a stack variable as a parameter. Since TOP is a discriminant of the type, we cannot modify it except by making an assignment to the entire record. PUSH and POP use a local variable named NEW__STACK for this purpose. When the procedures are called, NEW__STACK.TOP is initialized with the new value. The array NEW__STACK.DATA therefore has the new size. To return the new stack through S, then, the procedures simply set S equal to NEW__STACK.

Example 8.2

```
procedure PUSH(S : in out STACK; I : ITEM__TYPE) is
    NEW__STACK : STACK(S.TOP + 1);
begin
    NEW__STACK.DATA := S.DATA & I;
    S := NEW__STACK;
end PUSH;

procedure POP(S : in out STACK; I : out ITEM__TYPE) is
    NEW__STACK : STACK(S.TOP - 1);
```

```
begin
    if S.TOP = 0 then
        PUT("The stack is empty.");
    else
        I := S.DATA(S.TOP);
        NEW__STACK.DATA := S.DATA(1..S.TOP-1);
        S := NEW__STACK;
    end if;
end POP;
```

We can also represent stacks with access values. By creating access variables that designate other access variables, we can form a *linked list* of them. Each item in a linked list is a record composed of two parts: data components and a link component. The link component designates the next object in the list. Hence, if we have an access variable that designates the beginning of a list, we can follow its link components until we reach the end of the list. The last object in a linked list is marked by the access value *null*. Figure 8.2 shows the graphic notation in which linked lists are conventionally written.

Here is a declaration for a linked list that represents a stack:

```
type STACK2;
type STACK2__PTR is access STACK2;
type STACK2 is
    record
        DATA : ITEM__TYPE;
        NEXT : STACK2__PTR;
    end record;
TOP : STACK2__PTR;
```

To add a new item to the top of the stack, we now simply create a new object to contain it. The link component of the new object is then assigned the location of the item previously on top. Example 8.3 shows a procedure that performs this operation. It returns an access value designating the new top of the stack.

Example 8.3

```
procedure PUSH(S : in out STACK2__PTR; I : ITEM__TYPE) is
begin
    S := new (DATA => I, NEXT => S);
end PUSH;
```

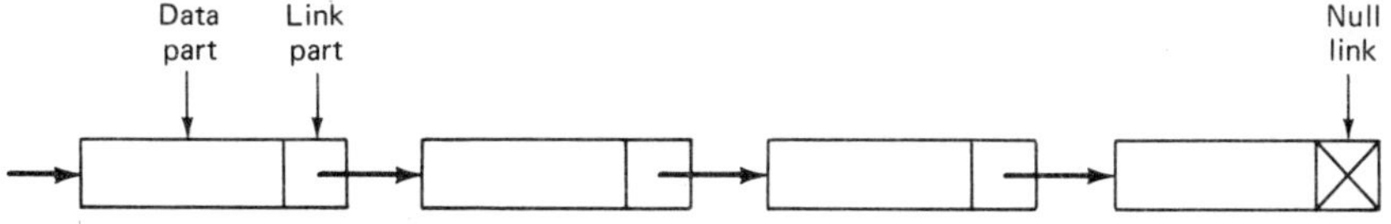

Figure 8.2: A linked list

Example 8.4 shows a procedure that performs the converse operation. Given an access variable designating the top of a stack, it returns the value of its data component and an access value designating the new top. To locate the new top, it simply takes the link component of the present top.

Example 8.4

```
procedure POP(S : in out STACK2__PTR; I : out ITEM__TYPE) is
begin
    if S = null then
        PUT("The stack is empty.");
    else
        I := S.all.DATA;
        S := S.all.NEXT;
    end if;
end POP;
```

POP assumes the top of the stack equals *null* when the stack is empty. This assumption is valid because the access value designating the top of the stack is initially *null*. As items are pushed onto the stack, a chain is formed that ends with the original *null* value. Example 8.5 shows a function that accepts an access value and follows the link component to the end, counting the number of items in the stack. Because it takes an *in* parameter, the function does not modify the stack or the top-of-stack designator.

Example 8.5

```
function STACK__SIZE(S : STACK2__PTR) return INTEGER is
    COUNT : INTEGER;
begin
    COUNT := 0;
    while S /= null loop
        S := S.all.NEXT;
        COUNT := COUNT + 1;
    end loop;
    return COUNT;
end STACK__SIZE;
```

As with the array representations, we cannot "pop" an item from an empty linked list. If we reference TOP.all (or one of its components) when TOP equals *null*, an error condition will result. In a program that uses these procedures, then, we might want to add a boolean function that determines whether a stack is empty.

8.4 LISTS AND TREES

In the previous section, we examined procedures for inserting and deleting at the base of a linked list. In this section, we look at subprograms that perform insertions, deletions, and searches of a more general nature. We also look at an access type representation for a data structure called the *binary tree*. Both linked lists and binary trees are useful when we want to maintain a collection of data in a particular order.

For instance, suppose we want to keep a collection of character strings in alphanumeric sequence. Suppose, also, that strings will be added and deleted. We would like to have a structure in which we can perform these operations conveniently, without upsetting the order of the strings. The declarations below define a linked list for this purpose:

```
type STR is STRING(1 .. 10);
type STR__LIST;
type STR__LIST__PTR is access STR__LIST;
type STR__LIST is
    record
        DATA : STR;
        NEXT : STR__LIST__PTR;
    end record;
BASE : STR__LIST__PTR;
```

Example 8.6 shows a procedure that prints the items (or *nodes*) in a linked list. It accepts a single parameter: an access value that designates the beginning (or *base*) of the list. It then follows the link components until it reaches one with the value *null*. This method was also employed by STACK__SIZE in example 8.5.

Example 8.6

```
procedure PRINT__LIST(L : STR__LIST__PTR) is
begin
    while L /= null loop
        PUT(L.all.DATA);
        L := L.all.NEXT;
    end loop;
end PRINT__LIST;
```

To insert a node in a linked list, we simply modify a few access values. The nodes themselves do not have to be moved. Say our list is a collection of surnames. Inserting the string "Johnson" between "Harris" and "Jones" changes the list as shown in figure 8.3. Importantly, the node containing "Johnson" does not have to be located between the other two. Since a linked list is a trail of access values, nodes that appear to be adjacent in the list need not be adjacent physically.

We can make this insertion with only two Ada statements. If BASE designates

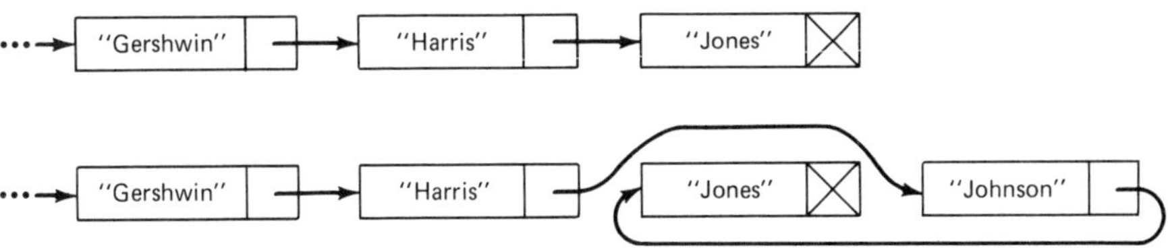

Figure 8.3: Linked list insertion

the node containing "Harris", and NEW__NODE designates the node containing "Johnson", then we can write

```
NEW__NODE.all.NEXT := BASE.all.NEXT;
BASE.all.NEXT := NEW__NODE;
```

Since "Jones" initially follows "Harris", BASE.all.NEXT initially designates the node containing "Harris". Thus, the first assignment forms a link from "Johnson" to "Jones". The second assignment forms a link from "Harris" to "Johnson". The chain is then complete. As it happens, we can compress the operation into a single assignment:

```
BASE.all.NEXT := new ("Johnson        ", BASE.all.NEXT);
```

The procedure shown in example 8.7 uses this method. It accepts a string and the base of a linked list. Unlike the procedure for stack insertion, which can add a node at only one position, this procedure can add to a list at its beginning, middle, or end. If the list is empty, the string is placed at the beginning of the list. Otherwise, the procedure uses an access variable named SEARCH__POS to follow the list until the string's proper position is found. (That is, it looks for the string's place in the alphabetic order of the list.) If the end of the list is reached first, the string is appended there.

Example 8.7

```
procedure INSERT(NEW__NAME : STR; BASE : in out STR__LIST__PTR) is
    SEARCH__POS : STR__LIST__PTR;
begin
    if BASE = null then      --is it empty?
        BASE := new (NEW__NAME,null);
    else
        SEARCH__POS := BASE;
        while (SEARCH__POS.all.DATA < NEW__NAME)
          and (SEARCH__POS.all.NEXT /= null) loop
              SEARCH__POS := SEARCH__POS.all.NEXT;
        end loop;
        SEARCH__POS.all.NEXT := new (NEW__NAME,SEARCH__POS.all.NEXT);
    end if;
end INSERT;
```

Deleting a node from a linked list involves the same kind of manipulation. Instead of physically obliterating the node, we simply rearrange the links to pass by it. To remove "Johnson" from the list we just created, we would modify BASE.all.NEXT as shown in figure 8.4.

The deletion can be made with one statement:

```
BASE.all.NEXT := BASE.all.NEXT.all.NEXT;
```

Example 8.8 shows a procedure for deleting from a linked list. It anticipates three cases. If the list is empty, it leaves FOUND equal to FALSE. If the first node

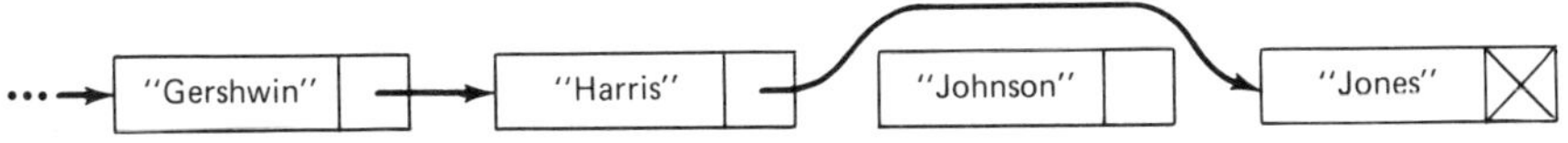

Figure 8.4: Linked list deletion

contains the name we want to delete, it sets FOUND to TRUE and deletes the node. Otherwise, it follows the links, stopping when it finds a match. If it reaches the end of the list without finding the given name, FOUND is again left FALSE.

Example 8.8

```
procedure DELETE(OLD__NAME : STR;
                 BASE : in out STR__LIST__PTR;
                 FOUND : out BOOLEAN) is
   --FOUND is returned true if the given name is
   --located in the list, false otherwise.
   SEARCH__POS : STR__LIST__PTR := BASE;
   NEXT__NODE : STR__LIST__PTR renames SEARCH__POS.all.NEXT;
begin
   FOUND := FALSE;
   if BASE = null then       --is the list empty?
      return;      --if so, then stop
   elsif BASE.all.DATA = OLD__NAME then
      BASE := NEXT__NODE;      --delete the first node
      FOUND := TRUE;
      return;
   else
      while NEXT__NODE /= null loop      --we have to search
         if NEXT__NODE.all.DATA = OLD__NAME then
            NEXT__NODE := NEXT__NODE.all.NEXT;
            FOUND := TRUE;
            return;
         end if;
      end loop;
   end if;
end DELETE;
```

Unlike a linked list, a binary tree is organized so that we can locate an item by examining only a few nodes. Each node in a binary tree includes *two* access values. One designates a "left" subtree and one designates a "right" subtree. To search a binary tree, we simply follow the subtree links. The starting point of a binary tree is called its *root*. Figure 8.5 shows a binary tree for our present application.

Binary trees have a variety of uses. Maintaining an ordered collection of strings is only one. We will use a particular kind of binary tree called a *search tree*. For each node of a binary search tree, we define its subtrees according to the string in the node. If a left subtree is present, it contains strings that are lexicographically smaller. If a right subtree is present, it contains strings that are lexicographically greater. The tree shown in figure 8.5 follows this schema.

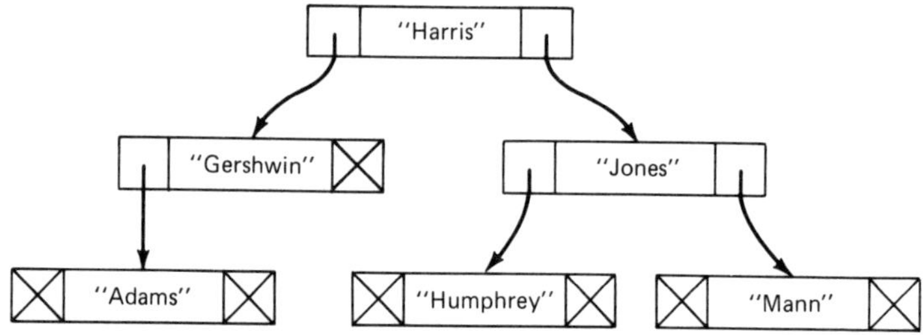

Figure 8.5: A binary tree

Here is a declaration sequence that forms a binary tree:

```
type STR is STRING(1 .. 10);
type TREE;
type TREE__PTR is access TREE;
type TREE is record
            DATA : STR;
            LEFT,RIGHT : TREE__PTR;
        end record;
ROOT : TREE__PTR;
```

To determine whether a string is present in a binary search tree, we use the properties of search trees to simplify the search. Instead of examining every node, we start at the root and then take either the left subtree or the right subtree at each stage. If the node we are examining contains the string we want, the search is over. If the node contains a string that is larger than ours, we go left; otherwise, we go right. Example 8.9 shows a recursive function for this purpose.

Example 8.9

```
function SEARCH(R : TREE__PTR; NAME : STR) return BOOLEAN is
begin
    if R = null then
        return FALSE;
    elsif R.all.DATA = NAME then
        return TRUE;
    elsif R.all.DATA > NAME then
        return SEARCH(R.all.LEFT,NAME);
    else
        return SEARCH(R.all.RIGHT,NAME);
    end if;
end SEARCH;
```

When nodes are inserted in a binary tree, they are always added along the bottom. Example 8.10 shows a function that accepts a tree and a string. It returns an access value designating a tree with the string in the proper position. The resemblance between ADD__TREE and SEARCH is not accidental. Both use the branching method outlined above. When ADD__TREE comes to a node at the bottom (or a *terminal node*), it attaches a new subtree to it.

Example 8.10

```
function ADD__TREE(R : TREE__PTR; NAME : STR) return TREE__PTR is
begin
    if R = null then       --is it a terminal node?
        return new (NAME,null,null) ;
    elsif R.all.DATA = NAME then
        return R ;      --the name is already there
    elsif R.all.DATA > NAME then
        R.all.LEFT := ADD__TREE(R.all.LEFT,NAME) ;
        return R ;
    else
        R.all.RIGHT := ADD__TREE(R.all.RIGHT,NAME) ;
        return R ;
    end if ;
end ADD__TREE ;
```

The process of "visiting" every node in a binary tree is called a *traversal*. To traverse a binary search tree in the relational order of its components, we follow three steps at each node, starting with the root. First, we traverse its left subtree, if one is present. Next, we "visit" the node itself. Finally, we traverse its right subtree. Example 8.11 shows a procedure that prints the nodes of a search tree alphabetically.

Example 8.11

```
procedure TRAVERSE(R : TREE__PTR) is
begin
    if R /= null then
        TRAVERSE(R.all.LEFT) ;
        PUT(R.all.DATA) ;
        TRAVERSE(R.all.RIGHT) ;
    end if ;
end TRAVERSE ;
```

Obviously, this section has sketched the use of linked lists and binary trees with rather broad strokes. We have given no attention here to the relative merits of these and other structures. Our purpose has instead been to show some access value manipulations. With these in hand, an Ada programmer can form data structures fitted to a particular application.

9

PACKAGES

9.1 PACKAGE DECLARATIONS

As we have seen, the declaration of a new data type specifies the domain of values it can represent. Yet this definition of a data type is seriously incomplete. A data type is not associated only with a domain of values: it is also associated with a collection of operations that can be performed on those values. The predefined type FLOAT, for instance, is associated with a collection of mathematical and logical operations on floating-point numbers.

To make this association more explicit, Ada allows us to write groups of related declarations in the form of a *package*. Any declaration that can appear in the declarative part of a program can appear inside a package declaration. The purpose of a package is to specify a data type and the subprograms that define its operations. Example 9.1 shows a package declaration that provides some facilities for complex numbers.

Example 9.1

```
package COMPLEX__MATH is
    type COMPLEX is record
                R : FLOAT ;      --real part
                I : FLOAT ;      --imaginary part
            end ;
    function "+"(X,Y : COMPLEX) return COMPLEX ;
    function "-"(X,Y : COMPLEX) return COMPLEX ;
    function "*"(X,Y : COMPLEX) return COMPLEX ;
    function "**"(X : COMPLEX ; I : INTEGER) return COMPLEX ;
    function CONV__FLOAT(F : FLOAT) return COMPLEX ;
end ;

package body COMPLEX is
    function "+"(X,Y : COMPLEX) return COMPLEX is
    begin
        return (X.R + Y.R, X.I + Y.I) ;
    end ;
```

```
    function "-"(X,Y : COMPLEX) return COMPLEX is
    begin
        return (X.R - Y.R, X.I - Y.I);
    end;
    .
    .
    .
    function CONV__FLOAT(F : FLOAT) return COMPLEX is
    begin
        return (R => F, I => 0.0);
    end CONV__FLOAT;
end COMPLEX__MATH;
```

The declaration has two parts. The first part is the specification, which gives the objects and data types that will be used in the package. It also gives the specifications of the subprograms in the package. The second part is the body, which gives the subprograms in their entirety. (In COMPLEX__MATH, some of the subprograms are named by overloaded operators.)

The specification is separated from the body in this way because the two perform different jobs. The specification provides the interface, while the body provides the implementation. To use the facilities in a particular package, all we need to know is the information given in the specification. This information includes the names of its subprograms and the parameters they take, along with the definition of the objects and types. In fact, we can feign that the body of a package is invisible from our view.

Ideally, we would like to treat a package as a "black box." That is, we would like to be able to use the subprograms in a package with no concern for their implementation. For that purpose, the information in the specification is sufficient.

A further distinction between the specification and the body can be made. The objects and types introduced in the specification can be referenced by other parts of the program, while those introduced in the body cannot. If we had introduced a variable in the body of COMPLEX__MATH, its scope would be restricted to the body. On the other hand, identifiers declared in the specification (such as the type COMPLEX) are available elsewhere. All the subprograms in COMPLEX__MATH fall into this category, because they appear first in the specification.

The identifiers declared in a package are directly visible in its specification and in its body. Here are some declarations that could appear in a subprogram of COMPLEX__MATH:

```
C1 : COMPLEX;
C2 : constant COMPLEX := (0.0, 0.0);
C3 : COMPLEX := CONV__FLOAT(-0.5);
```

Here are some assignments that might appear in such a subprogram:

```
C1 := (R => -1.0, I => 1.0e+5);
C3 := C3 + C2;
C1 := C3 ** 3;
```

Outside the package, but within its scope, the identifiers are hidden. They must therefore be qualified with the package name. Here is a declaration that might appear in a subprogram within the scope of COMPLEX__MATH:

```
C4 : COMPLEX__MATH.COMPLEX ;
```

Here is a possible assignment:

```
C4 := COMPLEX__MATH.CONV__FLOAT(3.1415) ;
```

We can also reference the components of C4, as below:

```
C4.I := C4.I/2 ;     --floating point divide
```

The need for qualification can be averted with a renaming declaration. Ada also allows us to make the identifiers in a package directly visible. In fact, we have been using this mechanism already: it is the *use* clause. If a package name is given in a *use* clause, the identifiers in its specification need not be qualified. Without a *use* clause, we would have to write statements like

```
TEXT__IO.GET(NUM) ;
TEXT__IO.PUT__LINE("Hello") ;
```

Use clauses can appear only in a declarative part. They are effective throughout the scope of the declarative part in which they appear. (If a *use* clause overloads an identifier, however, qualification may still be required for that identifier.) Example 9.2 shows how a *use* clause can make the subprograms in COMPLEX __MATH directly visible.

Example 9.2

```
with TEXT__IO; use TEXT__IO;
procedure SQUARE__COMPLEX is
    package COMPLEX__MATH is
      . . .     --from example 9.1
    end COMPLEX__MATH ;
    package FLT__IO is new FLOAT__IO(FLOAT) ;
    use FLT__IO,COMPLEX__MATH ;
    NUMBER : COMPLEX ;
begin
    PUT__LINE("Please enter the real part.") ;
    GET(NUMBER.R) ;
    PUT__LINE("Now enter the imaginary part.") ;
    GET(NUMBER.I) ;
    NUMBER := NUMBER ** 2 ;
    PUT("Squaring this number gives  ") ;
    PUT(NUMBER.R) ;
    PUT(" + ") ;
    PUT(NUMBER.I) ;
    PUT(" * i.") ;
    NEW__LINE ;
end SQUARE__COMPLEX ;
```

A variable declared in the body of a package is sometimes called an *own* variable of the package. Unlike variables that are local to a subprogram, an *own* variable is not destroyed between successive calls. Hence, it retains its value from one call to the next.

Additionally, the body of a package can include a sequence of statements to be executed when the package is elaborated. If a package appears in the declarative part of a function, for instance, the statement sequence in the package body will be executed before the body of the function itself. The purpose of a statement sequence in a package is to initialize variables (or devices) as needed by the subprograms in the package. Example 9.3 shows a package body with *own* variables and an initializing statement sequence. (Note that the same *end* terminates the statement sequence and the package.)

Example 9.3

```
package body IEEE__488 is
    A,B,PIA__STATUS : INTEGER;        --own variables
    procedure CONTROL__OUT is
    begin
       ...
    end CONTROL__OUT;
    function STATUS__IN return BOOLEAN is
    begin
       ...
    end STATUS__IN;
    procedure OUT__DEVICE__MESSAGE(STR : STRING) is
        COUNT : NATURAL;      --local
    begin
       ...
    end OUT__DEVICE__MESSAGE;
begin--initialization starts here
    MAKE__LISTENER;
    MAKE__TALKER;
    ENTER__STANDBY;
end IEEE__488;
```

If a package consists of object and type declarations, with no subprograms, then the body of the package can be omitted. A package of this kind might be used so a "pool" of related objects can be declared together. For example, we might write a package composed of string constant declarations that give the cursor control codes for a particular video terminal. In this way, we can keep the information needed to use the device in one place.

9.2 PRIVATE TYPES AND DEFERRED CONSTANTS

Just as Ada packages allow us to separate the specification of a subprogram from its body, we can also introduce types and constants separately from their full declarations. A type of this kind is said to be *private;* a constant of this kind is said to be *deferred*. Example 9.4 shows a package specification in which these features appear.

Example 9.4

```
package SYS__INFO is
    type ADDRESS is private;
    type NAME is private;
    MEMORY__SIZE : constant ADDRESS;
    SYSTEM__NAME : constant NAME;
private
    type ADDRESS is new INTEGER;
    type NAME is STRING(1 .. 10);
    MEMORY__SIZE : constant ADDRESS := 2 ** 24;
    SYSTEM__NAME : constant NAME := "Cyclone-Z  ";
end SYS__INFO;
```

The identifiers are introduced with incomplete declarations. Full declarations are then given in the *private part* of the specification. If a specification includes a private part, the declarations in the private part are preceded by the reserved word *private*. The type of a deferred constant must be a private type declared in the same package.

Within the package, a private type has all the properties of nonprivate types. If it is an array with a discrete component type, for example, the relational operators are defined for it. If it is a numeric type, the usual arithmetic operators are defined.

Outside the package, however, only a handful of operations can be applied to private types. First, variables of private types can be assigned values. Second, they can be tested for equality, inequality, and membership. (The other relational operators, such as "<=" and ">", are unavailable.) Third, they can be qualified and can appear in explicit type conversions. Finally, discriminants of variant records can be referenced by name. Other components of a record object cannot be referenced individually; neither can the components of an array object. We can define additional operations on objects of private types only by declaring subprograms for them in the package.

Example 9.5

```
package SETS is
    type SET is private;
    type ELEMENT is private;
    EMPTY__SET : constant SET;
    function "+"(A,B : SET) return SET;
    function "*"(A,B : SET) return SET;
    function "+"(S : SET; E : ELEMENT) return SET;
    function "+"(E : ELEMENT; S : SET) return SET;
    function MEMBER(S : SET; E : ELEMENT) return BOOLEAN;
private
    type ELEMENT is new INTEGER range 1 .. 256;
    type SET is array(ELEMENT) of BOOLEAN;
    EMPTY__SET : constant SET := (SET'RANGE => FALSE);
end;
package body SETS is
    function "+"(A,B : SET) return SET is
    begin
        return A or B;
    end;
```

```
    function "*"(A,B : SET) return SET is
    begin
        return A and B ;
    end ;
    function "+"(S : SET; E : ELEMENT) return SET is
        NEW__SET : SET ;
    begin
        NEW__SET := S ;
        NEW__SET(E) := TRUE ;
        return NEW__SET ;
    end ;
    function "+"(E : ELEMENT; S : SET) return SET is
    begin
        return S + E ;
    end ;
    function MEMBERS(S : SET; E : ELEMENT) return BOOLEAN is
    begin
        return S(E) ;
    end ;
end SETS ;
```

Example 9.5 shows a package that declares a data type and a collection of subprograms for sets. Within the private part of the specification, the set type is implemented as a boolean array. If a component of the array is TRUE, then the corresponding element is in the set. In the package body, three distinct operations are defined. The "+" operator gives the union of two sets; it can also be used to add a new element. The "*" operator gives the intersection of two sets. That is, it returns a set containing only the elements present in both operand sets. Finally, the MEMBER function returns TRUE if an element is in the given set, FALSE otherwise. Suppose these declarations follow the package:

```
use SETS ;
S1,S2 : SET ;
S3 : SET := EMPTY__SET ;
E1,E2 : ELEMENT ;
```

Here is an assignment that puts 5 in S3:

```
S3 := S3 + 5 ;
```

Other assignments might include

```
S2 := S3 + 200 ;
S1 := S2 * S3 ;
E1 := 17 ;
E2 := E1 mod 2 ;
S3 := (S1 * S2) + E2 ;
```

Here are some possible *if* statements:

```
if S2 = EMPTY__SET then ...
if S1 / = S3 then ...
if MEMBER(S2 + S3,41) then ...
```

The "+" operator names three subprograms in this package. The first takes two sets and combines them. The others take a set and an element. Two subprograms are needed for the second form so that the operation is commutative. One of them is for expressions like S1 + E1, while the other is for expressions like E1 + S1.

Between the introduction of a private type identifier and its full declaration, use of the identifier is restricted. During this interval, it can appear only in a deferred constant declaration, a type declaration, a subtype declaration, or a subprogram specification. It cannot appear in a variable declaration, for instance, or an allocator. This restriction also applies to subtypes of a private type and to composite types in which a private type is embedded.

9.3 LIMITED PRIVATE TYPES

We can enforce stricter isolation of private types by declaring them to be *limited.* Limited private types have all the properties of private types, with two additional restrictions. First, the equality and inequality operators are not implicitly defined for them. Second, variables with limited private types cannot be assigned values outside the package. Example 9.6 shows a package specification in which a limited private type for stacks is declared. (The package body could be filled in with example 8.2 as a guide.)

Example 9.6

```
package STACK__PKG is
    subtype ITEM__TYPE is STRING(1..64);
    type STACK(TOP : INTEGER := 0) is limited private;
    procedure PUSH(S : in out STACK; I : ITEM__TYPE);
    procedure POP(S : in out STACK; I : out ITEM__TYPE);
    function IS__EMPTY(S : STACK) return BOOLEAN;
private
    type STACK(TOP : INTEGER := 0) is
        record
            DATA : array(1..TOP) of ITEM__TYPE;
        end record;
end;
```

The only operations available on STACK are those given in the package. When we use STACK__PKG in a program, then, we can be confident that no "side effects" are changing the value of a stack outside the package. If STACK1 and STACK2 are of type STACK, then the following assignment is invalid outside of STACK__PKG:

```
STACK1 := STACK2;
```

Of course, assigning a value directly to S.TOP would be invalid whether STACK were private or not, because TOP is the discriminant of the record. As the package is written, incidentally, we cannot compare two stacks for equality or inequality. We could declare a subprogram for the "=" operator, if necessary. (Equality can be declared only for limited types. As noted in section 7.4, equality for other types cannot be redefined.)

A subprogram named by the "=" operator must be a function that takes two parameters of the same limited type and returns a boolean result. The "/=" operator cannot name a subprogram; inequality is automatically defined to give the converse of the equality function. Other relational operators can be overloaded for any type.

A composite type is limited if it has any limited components. A composite type can also be declared limited as in example 9.6. In either instance, aggregates are not available for composite types. Also, the catenation operator is unavailable for limited single-dimension arrays.

An additional restriction follows from the rules on limited types. In particular, objects with limited types cannot be given default initial values when they are declared or allocated. Initializing an object involves the assignment operator, which is unavailable for limited types outside the package.

9.4 LIBRARY PACKAGES

A number of predefined packages, or *library packages,* are available for use in Ada programs. Some are required by the language; others may be added by a particular implementation. Among the library packages in the first category, the most important are STANDARD and TEXT__IO. Their specifications are given in appendices C and D respectively.

A library package that is invoked by a program is said to be *included* in the program. STANDARD is included in every program. It introduces most of Ada's predefined identifiers and operators. These denote types (such as BOOLEAN and CHARACTER) and subprograms (such as *abs* and "**").

Other library packages must be invoked explicitly. A *with* clause is used for this purpose; it precedes the program header. In past chapters, we have used *with* to invoke TEXT__IO as shown below:

```
with TEXT__IO;
```

If we wanted to invoke a library package called FLOATING__TRIG as well, we would write

```
with TEXT__IO,FLOATING__TRIG;
```

We can view an Ada program as though it were preceded by the following "invisible" clauses:

```
with STANDARD;
use STANDARD;
```

To round out our discussion of private types, we will examine a library package called CALENDAR. This package defines some facilities that can be used to read the status of a system clock. Every implementation of Ada is required to have CALENDAR as given in the specification below.

```
package CALENDAR is
    type TIME is private ;
    subtype YEAR__NUMBER is INTEGER range 1901 .. 2099 ;
    subtype MONTH__NUMBER is INTEGER range 1 .. 12 ;
    subtype DAY__NUMBER is INTEGER range 1 .. 31 ;
    function CLOCK return TIME ;
    function YEAR(DATE : TIME) return YEAR__NUMBER ;
    function MONTH(DATE : TIME) return MONTH__NUMBER ;
    function DAY(DATE : TIME) return DURATION ;
    function SECONDS(DATE : TIME) return DURATION ;
    procedure SPLIT(DATE : TIME;
                    YEAR : out YEAR__NUMBER;
                    MONTH : out MONTH__NUMBER;
                    DAY : out DAY__NUMBER;
                    SECONDS : out DURATION) ;
    function TIME__OF(YEAR : YEAR__NUMBER;
                    MONTH : MONTH__NUMBER;
                    DAY : DAY__NUMBER;
                    SECONDS : DURATION := 0.0) return TIME ;
    TIME__ERROR : exception ;     --preview of coming attractions
    function "+"(LEFT : TIME; RIGHT : DURATION) return TIME ;
    function "+"(LEFT : DURATION; RIGHT : TIME) return TIME ;
    function "-"(LEFT : TIME; RIGHT : DURATION) return TIME ;
    function "-"(LEFT : DURATION; RIGHT : TIME) return TIME ;
    function "<"(LEFT,RIGHT : TIME) return BOOLEAN ;
    function "<="(LEFT,RIGHT : TIME) return BOOLEAN ;
    function ">"(LEFT,RIGHT : TIME) return BOOLEAN ;
    function ">="(LEFT,RIGHT : TIME) return BOOLEAN ;
private
    --implementation dependent
end ;
```

DURATION is a fixed-point type defined within STANDARD. A value of type DURATION gives a quantity of seconds. Though the range of DURATION varies from one version of Ada to another, it must permit magnitudes of at least one day. In other words, it must include the range -86400.0 . . 86400.0.

A value of type TIME gives the month, day, year, and seconds of a moment in time. This information is stored in some internal format, the details of which are unavailable to us. The subprograms given in the package allow conversion between standard notation and the internal one. TIME__OF takes a year, a month, a day, and a duration, returning the equivalent TIME value. YEAR, MONTH, DAY, and SECONDS take a value of type TIME and return the corresponding item. SPLIT returns all four.

Example 9.7

```
with TEXT__IO,CALENDAR; use TEXT__IO,CALENDAR;
procedure HOW__OLD is
    package INT__IO is new INTEGER__IO(INTEGER) ;
    use INT__IO ;
```

```
    BIRTH__YEAR : YEAR__NUMBER;
    BIRTH__MONTH : MONTH__NUMBER;
    YEAR__DIFF,MONTH__DIFF : INTEGER;
    NOW : TIME;
begin
    PUT__LINE("Please enter the year you were born.");
    GET(BIRTH__YEAR);
    PUT__LINE("Please enter the month you were born.");
    GET(BIRTH__MONTH);
    NOW := CLOCK;     --parameterless function
    NEW__LINE;
    if MONTH(NOW) > BIRTH__MONTH then
        MONTH__DIFF := MONTH(NOW) - BIRTH__MONTH;
        YEAR__DIFF := YEAR(NOW) - BIRTH__YEAR;
    else
        MONTH__DIFF := BIRTH__MONTH - MONTH(NOW);
        YEAR__DIFF := YEAR(NOW) - BIRTH__YEAR - 1;
    end if;
    PUT("You are now ");
    PUT(YEAR__DIFF);
    PUT(" years and ");
    PUT(MONTH__DIFF);
    PUT(" months old.");
end HOW__OLD;
```

Assuming that the machine has a clock of some kind, the function CLOCK returns its current status. Arithmetic operators can then be used to determine the interval between clock readings. (The relational operators for TIME refer to the times represented; for example, "March 1964" is greater than "June 1957.") Example 9.7 shows a program that accepts a person's birthday and reports his or her age. Since YEAR__NUMBER and MONTH__NUMBER are subtypes of INTEGER, they are used in INTEGER input–output statements here.

9.5 BENEFITS OF ISOLATION

It is tempting to use procedures and functions merely as convenient ways of avoiding redundancy. In this view, the primary benefit of subprograms is that they permit sequences of statements to be written only once when they would otherwise have to be duplicated throughout a program. By using subprograms to minimize duplication, a programmer can obviously write programs with fewer statements.

Although concision is a desirable benefit of subprograms, it is far from the most important. In large programs, the job of the programmer is complicated by a vast number of design details. These details often interact so that one design decision cannot be made without affecting another. Hence, the complexity of a programming project increases rapidly as it becomes more ambitious. By writing subprograms and packages that can be used as "black boxes," however, we can reduce the complexity of a program by dividing it into smaller parts. This result follows because subprograms and packages share a useful benefit: they allow us to isolate information.

When we say that a subprogram or a package "isolates" a piece of information, we mean that the information is hidden from other parts of the program. Broadly speaking, we can isolate three kinds of information: data type, algorithm, and environment. If the data type of an object is isolated within a package, then the rest of the program can be written with no concern for the implementation of the object. In example 9.1, all of the operations needed for the type COMPLEX are provided inside the package, so the implementation of COMPLEX can be ignored elsewhere. The fact that COMPLEX is implemented as a record is unimportant; if the package were later changed so that COMPLEX was an array type, no changes would be needed outside the package.

Private types allow this isolation to be enforced by the language. If COMPLEX were given as a private type, references to its record structure outside the package would be rejected. If COMPLEX were a limited private type, the enforcement would be stricter still. Though we can keep information about data types isolated without Ada's private type facility, isolation of private types is assured automatically.

If the algorithm used to perform an action is isolated, then other parts of the program can be written independently of it. A subprogram that affects other parts of the program is said to have *side effects*. An example of a subprogram with side effects is one that modifies a global variable. As noted in section 7.3, if a global variable is changed inside a subprogram, then the main program becomes dependent on the implementation of the subprogram, and vice versa.

If information about the environment is isolated to a subprogram or package, then other parts of the program can be written in a more general way. By "environment" we refer to the devices and other aspects of the system on which the program will run. If a program controls a plotting device, for example, we would want to isolate the low-level information needed to communicate with it. That is, we would want all interaction with the device to take place in a few subprograms, not throughout the program itself.

Keeping information isolated in this way offers several advantages. First, the resulting program is easier to read. If the body of a program is cluttered with information that is better relegated to subprograms and packages, a person who is reading it will have difficulty seeing what the program does. One way to look at this advantage is to distinguish the *logical* structure of a program from its *physical* structure. The logical structure of a program is simply the way the actions taking place in the program depend on one another; the physical structure of a program is the way it appears on paper. Using subprograms and packages for isolation makes the hierarchy of actions more apparent; that is, it makes the physical structure of a program more closely resemble its logical structure.

Second, the resulting program is easier to modify. If information about data types, algorithms, and environment is not isolated, then different parts of the program are forced to make assumptions about each other. Returning again to example 9.1, suppose that the record structure of COMPLEX was referenced outside the package. In that case, changing the implementation of COMPLEX would also require changes to the program outside. Hence, the programmer must contend with additional details each time a change is made. If all three kinds of isolation are maintained, on the other hand, then a modification in one part of the program will not surprise the programmer with new errors elsewhere.

Ease of modification is especially important in the area of environment. Since programs are sometimes moved to systems having different equipment or different software conventions, a program is more valuable if it can be adapted quickly and reliably. Programs that are easily adaptable to new environments are said to be *portable*. Isolation of environment information is essential for portability—particularly in large programs.

Finally, the resulting program is easier to write. A large programming project requires that the work of many people be coordinated. If a design decision affects many parts of the program, then decisions made by one programmer must be taken into account by other programmers. In this case, the efforts of the programmers must be coordinated more closely. The more each design decision can be isolated, the more independently each part of the effort can proceed. Subprograms and packages allow a program to be assembled from tested components that were produced by different people.

10

EXCEPTIONS

10.1 PREDEFINED EXCEPTIONS

Many kinds of error conditions can occur in a program. A user may enter an improper value; a programming mistake may cause a range constraint to be exceeded. When errors occur, Ada is often able to signal them. These signals are called *exceptions*. Each exception is denoted by an identifier. Raising an exception causes the flow of control to be interrupted.

As we will see in section 10.2, Ada allows us to provide statements that "handle" an exception. This way, we can have the program correct the error and then continue. If an exception is not handled within the program, then the program stops. In that case, the information in the program is lost.

Only a handful of exceptions are predefined by the language, so they are necessarily general. Some predefined exceptions are associated with *checks*, which are more specific. Five exceptions will be described here. Four are defined in STANDARD; one is defined in TEXT__IO. (Others are also defined, but they are related to more advanced features of the language.)

Of the exceptions defined in STANDARD, the first is CONSTRAINT__ERROR. It is associated with five checks. ACCESS__CHECK indicates an attempt to reference an object designated by a *null* access value. DISCRIMINANT__CHECK indicates an inconsistency concerning the discriminant of a composite value. INDEX__CHECK indicates an inconsistency concerning the bounds of an array, array slice, or index constraint. LENGTH__CHECK indicates an assignment, type conversion, or logical operation on arrays that do not have matching components. RANGE__CHECK indicates that a value is inconsistent with the range constraint of its type. It can also indicate that the range constraint of a subtype is incompatible with its base type.

NUMERIC__ERROR is raised by predefined arithmetic functions. DIVISION__CHECK indicates that a division-by-zero error has occurred in an expression with "/", *mod*, or *rem*. OVERFLOW__CHECK indicates that an expression has returned a value that is too large to be represented.

PROGRAM__ERROR is raised if a subprogram is called before its body has been elaborated. STORAGE__ERROR is raised if an allocator attempts to allocate an object when available memory space is insufficient. The corresponding checks are ELABORATION__CHECK and STORAGE__CHECK respectively.

Library package TEXT__IO defines DATA__ERROR. This exception is raised by GET if the input does not conform to the expected type. No check identifier is associated with it.

Since run-time error checking may entail an overhead, some implementations of Ada allow predefined exceptions to be suppressed. To give directives of this kind, we use language elements called *pragmas*. The pragma for suppressing predefined exceptions is denoted by the identifier SUPPRESS. Although different implementations can provide different pragmas, all implementations are required to accept SUPPRESS.

When we invoke the SUPPRESS pragma, we are giving permission for a particular run-time check to be omitted. This does not guarantee that the omission will actually be made, however. Some implementations have no provision for suppressing exceptions, in which case the pragma is ignored.

SUPPRESS pragmas should be given at the beginning of a declarative part. They take a check identifier as a parameter. Exceptions for which no check identifier is available cannot be suppressed. Since CONSTRAINT__ERROR is associated with more than one check identifier, on the other hand, we can omit either some of them or all of them. Here is a pragma that gives permission for ACCESS__CHECK to be omitted:

```
pragma SUPPRESS(ACCESS__CHECK);
```

SUPPRESS should not be used casually. Suppressing run-time error checking trades program reliability for efficiency. Since many errors in a program do not become apparent until after formal testing is completed, error checking serves a useful purpose even when a program is thought to be fully tested.

The scope of a SUPPRESS pragma is the same as the scope of declarations and clauses appearing in the same declarative part. Outside this region, the pragma has no effect. Hence, it might be applied to a small, time-critical subprogram without sacrificing reliability altogether.

10.2 HANDLING AN EXCEPTION

When an exception is raised, program control is transferred to an exception handler, if one has been provided. An exception handler is a sequence of statements that determines how the program will recover. Handlers can be placed at the end of a program, package, or subprogram. Example 10.1 shows a procedure that accepts an integer from the user; it includes a handler for DATA__ERROR exceptions.

Example 10.1

```
procedure GET__ACCOUNT(I : out INTEGER) is
begin
    PUT__LINE("Please enter your account number.");
    GET(I);
exception
    when DATA__ERROR =>
        PUT__LINE("Please enter an integer.");
        GET(I);
end GET__ACCOUNT;
```

If handlers are included, they are preceded by the reserved word *exception* to separate them from the rest of the body. The *when* construct used in handlers is similar to that used for branching and variant records. Here is an exception handler that could appear at the end of a subprogram called MULT__MATRICES:

```
exception
    when CONSTRAINT__ERROR =>
        PUT__LINE("The given matrices are incompatible.");
    when NUMERIC__ERROR =>
        PUT("An overflow or division-by-zero");
        PUT__LINE("has occurred.");
    when PROGRAM__ERROR | STORAGE__ERROR =>
        PUT__LINE("A programming error has been encountered.");
        PUT__LINE("Report this message to the computer center.");
end MULT__MATRICES;
```

As with branching uses of *when,* exception handlers can include an *others* clause. If an *others* clause is present, it will be executed in response to exceptions that are not listed elsewhere in the handler. In the preceding example, the last *when* choice could be replaced by an *others* clause; the warning message would then appear in response to any exception not already accounted for.

If an exception is raised in a subprogram that has no handler for it, the subprogram terminates. The exception is then raised again at the point where the subprogram was called. In this way, the caller is given an opportunity to handle the exception with its own handler. This process is termed *propagation*. Exceptions are propagated back to successive calling levels until a handler is found or until the main program must be terminated.

If another exception is raised inside a handler, the handler terminates. A handler for the new exception is then located, if possible. In example 10.1, a second DATA__ERROR exception would not cause the same handler to be executed again; the exception would instead be propagated to the place where GET__ACCOUNT was called.

Exceptions can also be raised during elaboration of a declarative part. If such an exception is raised in the declarative part of the main program, the program stops. If it is raised in the declarative part of a subprogram, the exception is propagated directly to the caller. Here is a declaration that might raise STORAGE_ERROR:

```
ADDR : INT_PTR := new INTEGER(16#FFF#);
```

An exception raised during the elaboration of a package has similar results. If the package appears in the declarative part of the main program, then the program stops. If the package is nested inside a subprogram, however, then the exception is propagated to the subprogram caller. Recall that the initializing statements in a package body are executed at elaboration time; as we have noted, a handler can be given for exceptions raised there.

10.3 RAISING AN EXCEPTION

We can declare identifiers for additional exceptions. These identifiers can denote error conditions that would not otherwise be recognized. For instance, a function that computes logarithms should signal an error condition if its parameter is less than or equal to zero. Since an exception of this kind is not defined by the language, we must declare it when we declare the function. Here are some exception declarations:

```
NEG_LOG : exception;
OVERFLOW,UNDERFLOW : exception;
```

The reserved word *exception* appears in these declarations to show that the identifiers represent exceptions. To raise a programmer-defined exception, we use the *raise* statement. Here is an *if* construct that might appear in a logarithm subprogram:

```
if X <= 0.0 then
    raise NEG_LOG;
end if;
```

An exception raised with *raise* has the same effect as a predefined exception raised by Ada's run-time checks. If the subprogram has a handler for NEG_LOG, control is transferred to the handler; otherwise, the exception is propagated. Hence, we can use exceptions to pass information from a subprogram to its caller. If a subprogram raises an exception, then the caller knows that an error condition occurred; if not, then the caller can assume the operation was successful.

Example 10.2

```
package STACK_PKG_2 is
    STACK_EMPTY,STACK_FULL : exception;
    subtype ITEM_TYPE is STRING(1..64);
    type STACK2 is limited private;
```

```
    type STACK2__PTR is access STACK2;
    procedure PUSH(S : in out STACK2__PTR; I : ITEM_____TYPE);
    procedure POP(S : in out STACK2__PTR; I : out ITEM__TYPE);
    function IS__EMPTY(S : STACK2__PTR) return BOOLEAN;
private
    type STACK2 is record
                DATA : ITEM__TYPE;
                NEXT : STACK2__PTR;
            end record;
end;
package body STACK__PKG__2 is
    procedure PUSH(in out STACK2__PTR; I : ITEM__TYPE) is
    begin
        S := new(DATA => I, NEXT => S);
    exception
        when STORAGE__ERROR =>        --predefined
            raise STACK__FULL;
    end PUSH;
    procedure POP(S : in out STACK2__PTR; I : out ITEM__TYPE) is
    begin
        if S = null then
            raise STACK__EMPTY;
        else
            I := S.all.DATA;
            S := S.all.NEXT;
        end if;
    end POP;
    function IS__EMPTY(S : STACK2__PTR) return BOOLEAN is
    begin
        return S = null      --a boolean expression
    end IS__EMPTY;
end STACK__PKG__2;
```

The package shown in example 10.2 uses a linked list representation of stacks, as in examples 8.3 and 8.4. Two exceptions are declared in the package. The first, STACK__FULL, is raised by PUSH if an additional item cannot be allocated. The second, STACK__EMPTY, is raised by POP if no items are left in the stack. Since PUSH and POP do not include handlers for these exceptions, they will be propagated to the caller when they are raised.

Ada's predefined exceptions can also be raised explicitly. Suppressing run-time checks has no effect on *raise*. This statement will raise STORAGE__ERROR, whether STORAGE__CHECK has been suppressed or not:

```
raise STORAGE__ERROR;
```

Within a handler, it may become apparent that an exception should be propagated further. To transfer control from one handler level to the next, we write a *raise* statement without an exception name. The exception is then raised again in the caller. This form of *raise* can appear only inside the handler of a subprogram. We can use it to perform a partial recovery in a subprogram, while still signaling to its caller that an error occurred.

10.4 EXCEPTIONS AND ROBUSTNESS

If Ada had no facilities to let us handle exceptions, then any error condition would cause a program to stop prematurely. If a user entered a number in invalid form, for instance, then the program would have no opportunity to ask for the number again. If a "divide-by-zero" error occurred, then the program would have no opportunity to recover. In cases like these, the program is sometimes said to *crash.*

Letting a program crash is obviously not desirable. This holds whether or not the error is one for which recovery is possible. Some examples of errors likely to fall in the first category are input errors and arithmetic errors, such as the ones mentioned above. Recovery from an input error is a simple matter of requesting the value again, perhaps with additional instructions. Some examples of errors likely to fall in the latter category are device errors, such as an attempt to use a printer that is not functioning or not available.

A program designed to prevent crashing is said to be *robust.* Ada's exception handling facilities are an important aid to robustness. Though some errors can be averted with extensive tests inside the program, others (such as input errors) cannot be caught in advance. They can be treated only after they have caused an exception to be raised. Ada programs can be made completely robust, because any error in an Ada program can be handled.

In this regard, we should set down two design principles. First, *Ada programs should never crash.* Again, allowing a program to crash is undesirable; in Ada, it is unnecessary. When a program crashes, a good deal of information is lost. The user loses not only the intermediate results that the program has calculated, but also all the information about the error itself. The cause of a crash is less difficult to find if the values of the relevant variables are available; the "post-mortem" information provided by the operating system may be too general to be of use.

Second, the response that a program makes to an error condition *should be determined at the highest possible level of the program.* In other words, exceptions should generally be propagated from the lowest levels of a program to the higher ones. For example, say we have a function that finds the factorial of the number. Rather than handling NUMERIC_ERROR exceptions inside the function, the function should propagate them to the caller. Though this rule may seem counter-intuitive, it offers two advantages. First, it makes the function more portable. We might prefer different kinds of recovery in different programs. If the function propagates the exception, we can choose different kinds of recovery without changing the function declaration. Second, it allows the recovery to be made by the part of the program that has the most information. The function knows only the number it was given, while the caller is able to take other things into account.

When an exception is finally handled, three kinds of recovery can be made. First, the program can simply ask the user to enter corrected values that will allow processing to continue. This is the most useful approach if the error was caused by invalid input. Second, the program can make reasonable assumptions about the error condition and correct it internally. This approach is sometimes taken in response to an arithmetic error. For instance, if an operation causes an overflow error—that is, if it yields a number that is too large for the machine to represent—then we might substitute a large valid number and proceed. (In cases like these, we would also give the user a warning message of some kind.) Third, the program can "die gracefully." That is, it can stop after giving the user a complete report about the error. If the error is thought to stem from a programming mistake, then the report should indicate values of key variables and the location in the program where the error occurred. If the error is thought to be the result of a user's mistake, on the other hand, then the report should inform the user of the actions that led to the error, as well as indicating how the error can be avoided.

11

GENERIC DECLARATIONS

11.1 INSTANTIATION AND FORMAL TYPES

Since subprogram identifiers can be overloaded, we can write different versions of a subprogram to perform the same operation on different kinds of data. To simplify the creation of multiple subprograms that share the same "template," Ada allows us to declare *generic* subprograms. A generic subprogram cannot be called; instead, it is used to form one or more subprograms that operate on different data types. Hence, generic subprograms save us the trouble of writing several declarations for nearly identical subprograms.

Packages can be written generically, too. An example of a generic package is INTEGER__IO, which is defined within library package TEXT__IO. Each time we instantiate INTEGER__IO, we are creating a new package. The new package is said to be an *instance* of the generic package. Here is an instantiation that creates an instance of INTEGER__IO called MY__IO__PKG:

```
package MY__IO__PKG is new INTEGER__IO(WEIGHT);
```

INTEGER__IO includes a number of subprograms, such as GET and PUT. Assuming that WEIGHT is a derived type of INTEGER, this declaration forms a package named MY__IO__PKG in which WEIGHT is used as the parameter type for GET and PUT. Here is part of the specification for INTEGER__IO:

```
generic
    type NUM is range <>;
package INTEGER__IO is
    procedure GET(ITEM : out NUM; in FIELD := 0);
    procedure PUT(ITEM : in NUM;
```

```
                    WIDTH : in FIELD := DEFAULT_FIELD;
                    BASE : in NUMBER_BASE := DEFAULT_BASE);
   end INTEGER_IO;
```

The identifier NUM is said to be a *formal type* of the package. When the package is instantiated, NUM will be associated with the given type. In this respect, instantiation is much like a subprogram call and NUM is much like a parameter. The designation *range* <> indicates that the actual type must be an integer type. (We will examine generic type associations for other types in the following section.)

Example 11.1

```
generic
   type ITEM_TYPE is range <>;
procedure SWAP(X,Y : in out ITEM_TYPE) is
   TEMP : ITEM_TYPE;
begin
   TEMP := X;
   X := Y;
   Y := TEMP;
end SWAP;
```

The generic subprogram in example 11.1 exchanges the values of two variables. It can be instantiated with an integer type, which is substituted for ITEM _TYPE in the resulting procedure. Here is a declaration that creates an instance of SWAP for the type INTEGER:

```
procedure INT_SWP is new SWAP(INTEGER);
```

Instantiations can be made in name notation as well as positional notation. This declaration is equivalent to the one above:

```
procedure INT_SWP is new SWAP(ITEM_TYPE => INTEGER);
```

After SWAP has been instantiated for a type, the resulting procedure can be called like any other. If J1 and J2 are variables of type INTEGER, the following call will exchange their values:

```
INT_SWP(J1,J2);
```

A generic declaration can take more than one formal type. The package shown in example 11.2 takes a pair of formal types. The first, INDEX, gives the index type of a square array type; the second, COMPONENTS, gives the component type of the array type. This array type is declared inside the package. Subprograms for arrays of this type are also provided.

Example 11.2

```
generic
   INDEX is range <>;
   COMPONENTS is range <>;
```

```
package MATRIX_ROUTINES is
    type MATRIX_TYPE is array(INDEX,INDEX) of COMPONENTS ;
    function DETERMINANT(M : MATRIX_TYPE) return FLOAT ;
    function "*"(M1,M2 : MATRIX_TYPE) return MATRIX_TYPE ;
    procedure INVERT(M : in out MATRIX_TYPE) ;
end ;
package body MATRIX_ROUTINES is
    ...
end MATRIX_ROUTINES ;
```

Here is a sequence of declarations that could follow MATRIX_ROUTINES:

```
subtype MY_INDEX is INTEGER range 1 .. 10 ;
subtype MY_COMPS is INTEGER range 0 .. INTEGER'LAST ;
package MR is new MATRIX_ROUTINES(MY_INDEX,MY_COMPS) ;
use MR ;
```

A *use* clause is included so that the identifiers declared in the specification of MR can be referenced without qualification. The instantiation can also be written this way:

```
package MR is new
        MATRIX_ROUTINES(COMPONENTS => MY_COMPS,INDEX =>
            MY_INDEX) ;
```

A package can also take a *formal object*. The package shown in example 11.3 takes a value of type POSITIVE and uses it in a type declaration. A default value can be given for a formal object; in this package, the default is 80. Here are some instantiations for MESSAGE_ROUTINES:

```
package M1 is new MESSAGE_ROUTINES(64) ;
package M2 is new MESSAGE_ROUTINES(LENGTH => 132) ;
package M3 is new MESSAGE_ROUTINES ;      --default is used
```

All three of these instantiations could appear in the same program. In this case, the identifiers declared inside the package would be overloaded. Since each instance of the package takes values whose types are easily distinguished, no ambiguity results. If an ambiguity did arise, then the subprogram and type names would have to be qualified with their package names. For instance, we might write M2.SEND to specify a particular instance of SEND.

Example 11.3

```
generic
    LENGTH : POSITIVE := 80 ;
package MESSAGE_ROUTINES is
    type STR is STRING(1 .. LENGTH) ;
    procedure ENCODE(S : in out STR) ;
    procedure DECODE(S : in out STR) ;
    procedure SEND(S : STR) ;
    procedure RECEIVE(S : out STR) ;
end ;
```

```
package body MESSAGE_ROUTINES is
    ...
end MESSAGE_ROUTINES;
```

11.2 TYPE MATCHING

In the previous section, we used the designation *range* <> for integer formal types. Here are the designations used for other scalar formal types:

```
digits <>        --floating point
delta <>         --fixed point
(<>)             --discrete
```

The designation for discrete types is "upward compatible" with that for integer types. A formal type defined with *(<>)* can be matched with integer types and enumeration types (including character types). The discrete type designation, however, restricts the operations available for the type within the generic body. A discrete formal type can be manipulated only with the discrete type operations, such as SUCC and PRED. The arithmetic operations defined for integers are unavailable for discrete formal types, even if an integer type is given in the instantiation.

Example 11.4

```
generic
    type FLOATER is digits <>;
package TRIG_FUNCTIONS is
    function SIN(ANGLE : FLOATER) return FLOATER;
    function COS(ANGLE : FLOATER) return FLOATER;
    function TAN(ANGLE : FLOATER) return FLOATER;
    function ARCTAN(X : FLOATER) return FLOATER;
end;
package body TRIG_FUNCTIONS is
    ...
end TRIG_FUNCTIONS;
```

The package shown in example 11.4 must be instantiated with a floating point type. Inside the package, the operations available for FLOATER values are those defined for floating point types. Attribute enquiries can be used in the package body to determine characteristics of the type.

Array types can be formal types, as well. If a formal array type is constrained, then the actual type must be constrained, and conversely. Here is a sequence of formal type declarations for a constrained array type:

```
type INDEX is (<>);
type F is digits <>;
type LIST1 is array(INDEX) of F;
```

An instantiation for the subprogram or package that includes these declarations must give a constrained array type with a floating-point component type. The array types NUMBERS and TRIG__VALUES declared below meet this requirement:

```
type NUMBERS is array (1 .. 100) of FLOAT;
type RADIANS is digits 6;
type TRIG__VALUES is array ('A' .. 'D') of RADIANS;
```

Here is a sequence that defines an unconstrained formal array type:

```
type INDEX is (<>);
type F is digits <>;
type LIST2 is array (INDEX range <>) of F;
```

Within the subprogram or package, an object of type LIST2 would have to be constrained in its declaration. The actual type must be unconstrained. Here is a type that could be matched with LIST2 in an instantiation:

```
type UNCONSTR is array(CHARACTER range <>) of FLOAT;
```

Example 11.5 shows a generic procedure that takes a contrained array type. The procedure uses nested *for* loops to set all the components of a two-dimension array to zero. Within the body of the procedure, the bounds of the actual type are determined by attribute enquiries.

Example 11.5

```
generic
    type INDEX1 is (<>);
    type INDEX2 is (<>);
    type COMPS is range <>;
    type SQUARE is array(INDEX1,INDEX2) of COMPS;
procedure ZERO(S : in out SQUARE) is
begin
    for I in S'RANGE(1) loop
        for J in S'RANGE(2) loop
            S(I,J) := 0;
        end loop;
    end loop;
end ZERO;
```

Other types can be matched as private types. A private formal type can match any type, scalar or composite. Within a generic body, a private formal type has only the properties of private types described in section 9.2. (An actual type that is limited cannot match a formal type unless the formal type is also limited.) Example 11.6 shows the specification for a stack package that can be instantiated for stacks with any item type.

Example 11.6

```
generic
    type ITEM_TYPE is private ;
package GEN_STACK_PKG is
    STACK_EMPTY,STACK_FULL : exception ;
    type STACK(TOP : INTEGER := 0) is limited private ;
    procedure PUSH(S : in out STACK; I : in ITEM_TYPE) ;
    procedure POP(S : in out STACK; I : out ITEM_TYPE) ;
    function IS_EMPTY(S : STACK) return BOOLEAN ;
private
    type STACK(TOP : INTEGER := 0) is
        record
            DATA : array(1 .. TOP) of ITEM_TYPE ;
        end record ;
end ;
```

The component type of a formal array type can be designated as a private type. In this case, the components of the array type are subject to private type rules. Here is a sequence of declarations for a formal type that can be matched with any single-dimension constrained array type:

```
type INDEX is (<>) ;
type COMPS is private ;
type MATRIX is array(INDEX) of COMPS ;
```

Assuming that the above sequence is taken from a generic procedure named REVERSE, we can write an instantiation like this one:

```
type SUBSCR is INTEGER range 1 .. 24 ;
type REC is record
                NAME : STRING(1 .. 20) ;
                PHONE : STRING(1 .. 10) ;
            end record ;
type REC_LIST is array(SUBSCR) of REC ;
procedure REC_LIST_REVERSE is new REVERSE(SUBSCR,REC,REC_LIST) ;
```

A formal type can be given an access type definition. In this case, the type that the access type designates must be the same for the actual type as for the formal type. Here is a pair of declarations that could appear in a generic declaration:

```
type BASE is private ;
type TREE is access BASE ;
```

If these declarations appeared in a procedure named TRAVERSE, we could write this instantiation:

```
type BINARY ;
type BINARY_PTR is access BINARY ;
type BINARY is record
```

```
                DATA : STRING(1 .. 10);
                LEFT,RIGHT : BINARY__PTR;
            end record;
   procedure BIN__TRAV is new TRAVERSE(BINARY,BINARY__PTR);
```

11.3 SUBPROGRAM MATCHING

Suppose we have a generic subprogram for sorting an array. To sort the components of an array, we must have relational operators for the component type. If the component type is a scalar type or a single-dimension array, then no additional provisions are needed. If the component type is one for which the relational operators are not defined, however, we must give information about the relational ordering of the type when the subprogram is instantiated.

For situations like these, Ada allows generic declarations to accept *formal subprograms*. Example 11.7 shows a procedure that uses a primitive sorting method to sort the components of an array with any component type and any discrete index type. An instantiation of SORT must give the name of a boolean function for comparing two values of the component type.

Example 11.7

```
generic
    type INDEX is (<>);
    type COMPS is private;
    with function ">"(X,Y : COMPS) return BOOLEAN;
    type LIST is array(INDEX) of COMPS;
procedure SORT(L : in out LIST) is
    THIS,NEXT : INDEX;
    SWAP : COMPS;
    SORTED : BOOLEAN := FALSE;
begin
    while not SORTED loop
        SORTED := TRUE;
        for THIS in INDEX'FIRST .. INDEX'PRED(INDEX'LAST) loop
            NEXT := INDEX'SUCC(THIS)
            if L(THIS) > L(NEXT) then       --supplied function
                SWAP := L(THIS);
                L(THIS) := L(NEXT);
                L(NEXT) := SWAP;
                SORTED := FALSE;
            end if;
        end loop;
    end loop;
end SORT;
```

The actual subprogram can be specified with an identifier or an operator symbol. Here is a sequence of declarations that instantiates SORT:

```
type I is INTEGER range 1 .. 100;
type C is record
```

```
                    FIRST__NAME,LAST__NAME,TITLE : STRING(1 .. 10);
                end record;
    type NAME__DIR is array(I) of C;
    function GT(P,Q : C) return BOOLEAN is
    begin
        if P.LAST__NAME > Q.LAST__NAME then
            return TRUE;
        else
            return FALSE;
    end;
    procedure SORT__REC is new SORT(INDEX => I, COMPS => C,
                                    ">" => GT, LIST => NAME__DIR);
```

Since GT compares two records of type C according to the LAST__NAME field, SORT will order records of an array accordingly. A formal subprogram can take parameters of any types. In the case of GT, the parameter type is the actual type corresponding to COMPS. Parameter types of formal subprograms can also be given as ordinary type names, as shown in example 11.8. SIGMA takes the bounds of an integer range and returns the sum of the values of the actual function in the range. If SIGMA were instantiated under the name SUM__OF__SQRS for a function that returns the square of an integer, then SUM__OF__SQRS(1,3) would return 1+2+9, or 12.

Example 11.8

```
generic
    with function FUNC(F : INTEGER) return INTEGER;
function SIGMA(START,FINISH : INTEGER) return INTEGER is
    SUM : INTEGER := 0;
begin
    for I in START .. FINISH loop
        SUM := SUM + FUNC(I);
    end loop;
    return SUM;
end SIGMA;
```

A default can be given for a formal subprogram. In this case, the corresponding item can be omitted from the instantiation. The formal subprogram specified below is matched with an actual subprogram named TO__SCREEN if no other choice is given in the instantiation:

```
with procedure OUT__CHAR(CH : in CHARACTER) is TO__SCREEN;
```

A default can be specified with a box symbol ("<>") if the default subprogram has the same name as the formal subprogram. In this case, a matching subprogram must be visible at the point where the declaration is instantiated. This formal subprogram is matched with an actual subprogram named SAMPLE by default:

```
with procedure SAMPLE(PT : out TEN__BITS) is <>;
```

Formal subprograms, like formal types, are aids to modularity. Instead of writing and testing a large number of duplicative subprogram and package declarations, we can write a single generic declaratiron that operates on a variety of types and their associated subprograms. In this way, Ada allows the "hands off" advantages of subprograms to be extended further.

12

FILES

12.1 TEXT FILE FORMATTING

We can think of a file variable as a "window" between a program and an external device. By performing operations on a file variable, we can communicate with devices that collect, transmit, and store data. Each file variable has a component type that determines the data type of its contents. In the programs we have seen so far, input and output has involved only *text files*. A text file is a file with a character or string component type.

In the next section, we will see the procedures used to associate a device with a file variable. In this section, we will continue to use only the default device, which is assumed to be a keyboard terminal of some kind. As we have seen, the package TEXT__IO provides facilities for text file input–output. These facilities include input–output subprograms for character and string types, along with a handful of generic packages that provide input–output subprograms for other types. The specification part of TEXT__IO is given in appendix D.

Predeclared text file subprograms include GET, PUT, NEW__LINE, GET__LINE, and PUT__LINE, described in sections 1.4 and 5.4. Additional subprograms are provided to simplify formatting. These subprograms can be called with or without a file variable parameter. If no file variable is given, the default is assumed.

Ada maintains three counts for each text file: the current column number, the current line number, and the current page number. These counts have the type POSITIVE__COUNT, defined as follows:

```
type COUNT is range 0 .. implementation defined;
type POSITIVE__COUNT is COUNT range 0 .. COUNT'LAST;
```

The function COL returns a value of type POSITIVE__COUNT indicating the current column. The procedure SET__COL takes a value of type POSITIVE

__COUNT and moves the cursor or printhead to the desired position. The procedure SET__LINE__LENGTH takes a value of type COUNT and sets the maximum line length accordingly. The function LINE__LENGTH, conversely, returns the present limit. If a text file has a maximum line length, then output that would exceed the limit is carried over to the next line. If the lines of a text file are unbounded, on the other hand, then no such checking occurs. Giving SET__LINE__LENGTH a value of 0 indicates that the line length should be unbounded. LINE__LENGTH returns 0 if the file has unbounded lines. (Text files have unbounded lines initially.)

The function LINE returns the current line number. The procedures SET__LINE calls NEW__LINE until the line number counter equals the given value. If the line number counter already equals the given value, no action takes place. If the line number counter is less than the given value, then the print position is moved to the indicated line on the following page. SET__PAGE__LENGTH and PAGE__LENGTH set and report the maximum number of lines per page. As with column limits, the line limit of a text file is initially 0, indicating that the pages have unbounded lengths. The exception LAYOUT__ERROR is raised if SET__COL or SET__LINE select a position that exceeds the current limits.

For pages, the function PAGE returns the current page number. NEW__PAGE is analogous to NEW__LINE; it causes subsequent output to appear on the following page of the file. The number of pages in a file is bounded only by the physical limitations of the external device.

Example 12.1

```
UNBOUNDED,TOO__BIG : exception ;
procedure CENTER(S : STRING) is
    PLACE : POSITIVE__COUNT ;
begin
    if LINE__LENGTH = 0 then
        raise UNBOUNDED
    elsif LINE__LENGTH < S'LENGTH then
        raise TOO__BIG ;
    else
        PLACE := (LINE__LENGTH - S'LENGTH)/2 ;
        SET__COL(PLACE) ;
        PUT(S) ;
    end if ;
end CENTER ;
```

The procedure shown in example 12.1 prints a string in the center of the current line. Once the starting position of the string is calculated, SET__COL moves the cursor or printhead to that column. Two exceptions are also declared. UNBOUNDED is raised if the file has unbounded line lengths; in this case, the procedure has no way to determine the center of a line. TOO__BIG is raised if the string is larger than the limit set for the lines. The exceptions are declared outside the procedure so that their scope will include any statements that call the procedure.

Example 12.2

```
with TEXT__IO; use TEXT__IO;
procedure POWERS__TABLE is
    --This program prints a table of the numbers from 1 to 20,
    --along with their squares and cubes.
    package INT__IO is new INTEGER__IO(INTEGER);
    use INT__IO;
begin
    NEW__PAGE;        --start at beginning of next page
    PUT("--N--");
    SET__COL(10);
    PUT("-- N**2 --");
    SET__COL(20);
    PUT("-- N**3 --");
    NEW__LINE;
    for N in 1..20 loop
        PUT(N);
        SET__COL(10);
        PUT(N**2);
        SET__COL(20);
        PUT(N**3);
        NEW__LINE;
    end loop;
end POWERS__TABLE;
```

The program shown in Example 12.2 uses SET__COL to print numbers in tabular form. Short headers are placed above each column of numbers. The first column starts in print column 0; the second starts in print column 10; the third starts in print column 20. NEW__LINE is used to start printing at column 0 after each line is completed.

12.2 FILE MANAGEMENT

As noted in the previous section, a file variable must be associated with an external device. Mass storage devices are usually organized in such a way that a file variable must be associated with a particular pool of data within the device. These pools of data are sometimes called *external files;* to avert confusion, we will call them *datasets*. The action of associating a file variable with a device or a dataset is termed *opening* the file. A file that is not associated with a device or a dataset is said to be *closed*.

The component type of a file is not specified when the file variable is declared. Instead, file variables are declared to have the type FILE__TYPE. For text input–output, the component type is automatically CHARACTER. In later sections we will examine operations involving files with other component types.

Every file variable is also associated with a *mode* indicating whether the file is to be used for input or output. These modes are represented by an enumeration type named FILE__MODE. A file with the mode IN__FILE can be used only for input. A file with the mode OUT__FILE can be used only for output. For terminal input–output, the terminal is typically viewed as a pair of files: one of mode IN __FILE for the keyboard and one of mode OUT__FILE for the display.

Ada provides two procedures for opening a file. Both take four parameters: the name of the file variable, the mode of the file, the system name of the device or dataset, and the system options desired, if any. The format of the last two items depends on the operating system under which the program is running. Different operating systems have different requirements concerning the formation of device and dataset names. For text files, the file-opening procedures have the following specifications:

```
procedure CREATE(FILE : in out FILE__TYPE;
                 MODE : in FILE__MODE := OUT__FILE;
                 NAME : in STRING := "";
                 FORM : in STRING := "";
procedure OPEN(FILE : in out FILE__TYPE;
                 MODE : in FILE__MODE;
                 NAME : in STRING;
                 FORM : in STRING := "");
```

CREATE should be used to open a file if it is to be associated with a device or a new dataset. OPEN should be used if the file is to be associated with a dataset that already exists. The default NAME parameter for CREATE is the null string, which indicates that the file variable should be associated with a temporary dataset. A temporary dataset exists only while the program is running; it is not accessible after the program stops.

Several exceptions can be raised by these procedures. STATUS__ERROR is raised if the program attempts to open a file variable that is already open. USE__ERROR is raised if a file is associated with a device that is incompatible with the given mode. For instance, USE__ERROR would be raised if a file of mode IN__FILE were associated with an output-only device or vice versa. NAME__ERROR is raised if the NAME parameter does not give a legal device or dataset name. OPEN can also raise NAME__ERROR if the given name indicates a dataset that does not exist. These exceptions can be raised in other circumstances as defined by the implementation.

Once a text file has been opened, it can be used with the predefined input–output subprograms, such as GET and PUT. The file variable is simply an additional parameter of the subprograms, as the specifications in appendix D show. The procedure in example 12.3 uses TEXT__IO subprograms to test an output device. The procedure places a short test pattern on each line of the first page. Since GET__LINE is used to read the device name, a variable of type NATURAL is supplied to store its length. GET__LINE will place the length of EXTERNAL__ID in LEN when it is read. Later references to the device name are made with the slice EXTERNAL__ID(1 . . LEN).

Example 12.3

```
procedure TEST__PRINT is
    EXTERNAL__ID : STRING(1..10);
    LEN : NATURAL;
    MY__FILE : FILE__TYPE;
```

```
begin
    PUT_LINE("Enter the name of the device.");
    GET_LINE(EXTERNAL_ID, LEN);
    CREATE(MY_FILE, OUT_FILE, EXTERNAL_ID(1..LEN));
    SET_LINE_LENGTH(MY_FILE, 80);
    SET_PAGE_LENGTH(MY_FILE, 66);
    while LINE(MY_FILE) < LINE_LENGTH(MY_FILE) loop
        for CHAR in 'A'..'Z' loop
            PUT(MY_FILE,CHAR);
        end loop;
        NEW_LINE(MY_FILE);
    end loop;
end TEST_PRINT;
```

The default input and output files can be changed as the program runs. Procedure SET_INPUT accepts a text file variable and causes it to be the new default file; SET_OUTPUT does the same for the default output file. Conversely, functions CURRENT_INPUT and CURRENT_OUTPUT return a value of type FILE_TYPE indicating the current defaults. The following statements therefore have the same effects:

```
PUT("Hello.");
PUT(CURRENT_OUTPUT, "Hello.");
```

Functions STANDARD_INPUT and STANDARD_OUTPUT return the files defined by the implementation as the defaults when the program starts. Unless SET_INPUT or SET_OUTPUT are called, these functions will return the same values as CURRENT_INPUT and CURRENT_OUTPUT. Here is a sequence of statements that opens a file, makes it the default output file, prints a line onto it, and then sets the default file back to the standard:

```
CREATE(NEW_CONSOLE,OUT_FILE,"TTA2:");
SET_OUTPUT(NEW_CONSOLE);
PUT_LINE("We are printing on device TTA2.");
SET_OUTPUT(STANDARD_OUTPUT);
```

Ada provides the RESET procedure so we can backtrack over a file that the program has already read or written. When RESET is called, the page, line, and column counts of the file are set to 1. RESET also allows us to give a file a new mode. Exception STATUS_ERROR is raised by RESET if the file is not open. If no mode parameter is given, RESET leaves the file with its previous mode. Here are the specifications for the two forms of RESET:

```
procedure RESET(FILE : in out FILE_TYPE);
procedure RESET(FILE : in out FILE_TYPE;
                MODE : in FILE_MODE);
```

Two procedures are provided for closing files. Both accept a parameter of type FILE_TYPE. Procedure DELETE expects to be given a dataset, which it closes and then deletes from the device. Procedure CLOSE can be given any file variable, which it simply closes. If a file is not closed before the program stops, the status of the device or dataset depends on the Ada implementation.

Ada also provides four functions that give information about a file variable. IS__OPEN returns TRUE if the given file is open, FALSE otherwise. MODE returns a value of type FILE__MODE indicating the current mode of the file. NAME returns a string containing the system name of the device or dataset. FORM returns a string containing other system information about the file. MODE, NAME, and FORM raise STATUS__ERROR if the given file is not open.

12.3 SEQUENTIAL FILE OPERATIONS

The library package TEXT__IO provides subprograms for use with text files. To access files with other kinds of components, we use a generic library package named SEQUENTIAL__IO. Although file variables accessed with TEXT__IO are technically sequential files as well, we will reserve the term *sequential file* for files that are accessed with instances of SEQUENTIAL__IO.

No default sequential files are defined. Hence, SEQUENTIAL__IO does not provide subprograms such as CURRENT__INPUT and CURRENT__OUTPUT. Otherwise, it provides the same file management subprograms as TEXT__IO, including CREATE, OPEN, CLOSE, DELETE, RESET, MODE, NAME, FORM and IS__OPEN. Their usage is the same for sequential files as for text files.

Unlike TEXT__IO, which is an actual package, SEQUENTIAL__IO must be instantiated. For each data type that is to be used as a component type, one instance of SEQUENTIAL__IO must be created. Here is a series of statements that declares a file variable with record components:

```
type AUTO is record
                  MAKE,MODEL : STRING(1 .. 20)
                  YEAR : INTEGER range 1 .. 2999 ;
                  LICENSE : STRING(1 .. 6) ;
             end ;
package AUTO__IO is new SEQUENTIAL__IO(AUTO) ;
AUTO__FILE : AUTO__IO.FILE__TYPE ;
```

Many of the identifiers in AUTO__IO are overloaded, for they also appear in TEXT__IO and in other instances of SEQUENTIAL__IO. Instances of SEQUENTIAL __IO can appear in *use* clauses, of course, but full qualification may be preferable for readability. In the declarations above, FILE__TYPE must be qualified to distinguish it from the FILE__TYPE declared in TEXT__IO and elsewhere. Here is a statement that opens AUTO__FILE:

```
AUTO__IO.CREATE(AUTO__FILE,OUT__FILE,"CARS.DATA") ;
```

The procedures for sequential file input–output are READ and WRITE. Their effects are analogous to those of GET and PUT respectively. The principal difference is that GET and PUT represent values in their legible character form, while READ and WRITE use an internal coding that varies from one implementation to another. Here are the specifications for the READ and WRITE procedures in AUTO__IO:

```
AUTO__IO.READ(FILE : AUTO__IO.FILE__TYPE;
                    ITEM : out AUTO);
AUTO__IO.WRITE(FILE : AUTO__IO.FILE__TYPE ;
                    ITEM : in AUTO);
```

The program shown in example 12.4 accepts floating point numbers from the user and places them in a sequential file. Note that the program uses four packages for input–output. TEXT__IO is used for prompting and for reading the dataset name. TEXT__INT, an instance of INTEGER__IO, is used to read the number of items in the user's list. TEXT__FLT is used to read the items. (Recall that INTEGER__IO and FLOAT__IO are generic packages embedded in TEXT__IO.) Finally, SEQ__FLOAT is an instance of SEQUENTIAL__IO used for writing the floating point numbers to the file.

Example 12.4

```
with TEXT__IO,SEQUENTIAL__IO; use TEXT__IO;
procedure STORE__FLOATS ;
    SIZE : INTEGER ;
    NUMBER : FLOAT ;
    EXT__NAME : STRING(1 .. 12) ;
    LEN : NATURAL ;
    package SEQ__FLOAT is new SEQUENTIAL__IO(FLOAT) ;
    package TEXT__INT is new INTEGER__IO(INTEGER) ;
    package TEXT__FLT is new FLOAT__IO(FLOAT) ;
    MY__FILE : SEQ__FLOAT.FILE__TYPE ;
    use TEXT__INT,TEXT__FLT ;
begin
    PUT__LINE("What is the name of the dataset?") ;
    GET__LINE(EXT__NAME,LEN) ;
    PUT("How many numbers do you want to store in ") ;
    PUT(EXT__NAME(1..LEN)) ;
    PUT__LINE("?") ;
    GET(SIZE) ;
    SEQ__FLOAT.CREATE(MY__FILE, OUT__FILE, EXT__NAME(1..LEN)) ;
    for I in 1..SIZE loop
        GET(NUMBER) ;
        SEQ__FLOAT.WRITE(MY__FILE, NUMBER) ;
    end loop ;
end STORE__FLOATS ;
```

The END__OF__FILE function accepts a file name and returns a boolean value to indicate whether the end of the file has been reached. STATUS__ERROR is raised if the file is not open; MODE__ERROR is raised if the mode of the file is not IN__FILE. The procedure shown in example 12.5 accepts an open file with components of type AUTO and prints them. It raises an exception named PRINT __ERROR if the file cannot be printed.

Example 12.5

```
PRINT__ERROR : exception ;
procedure PRINT__AUTOS(F : AUTO__IO.FILE__TYPE) is
    ONE__REC : AUTO ;
    use AUTO__IO ;
begin
    if not IS__OPEN(F) then
        raise PRINT__ERROR ;
    elsif MODE(F) /= IN__FILE then
        raise PRINT__ERROR ;
    else
        RESET(F) ;      --start at the beginning
        while not END__OF__FILE(F) loop
            READ(F,ONE__REC) ;
            NEW__LINE ;      --extra line between entries
            PUT__LINE(ONE__REC.MAKE) ;
            PUT__LINE(ONE__REC.MODEL) ;
            PUT(ONE__REC.YEAR) ;
            PUT(" ") ;
            PUT__LINE(ONE__REC.LICENSE) ;
        end loop ;
    end if ;
end PRINT__AUTOS ;
```

The procedure in example 12.5 makes AUTO__IO visible by placing it in a *use* clause. The procedure in example 12.6, on the other hand, references identifiers from AUTO__IO in their fully qualified form. The procedure accepts the names of two datasets and copies the first onto the second. It then closes the files.

Example 12.6

```
procedure COPY__AUTO__FILES(NAME1,NAME2 : STRING) is
    SOURCE,DEST : AUTO__IO.FILE__TYPE ;
    R : AUTO ;
begin
    AUTO__IO.OPEN(SOURCE,NAME1,IN__FILE) ;
    AUTO__IO.CREATE(DEST,NAME2,OUT__FILE) ;
    while not AUTO__IO.IS__OPEN(SOURCE) loop
        AUTO__IO.READ(SOURCE, R) ;
        AUTO__IO.WRITE(DEST, R) ;
    end loop ;
    AUTO__IO.CLOSE(SOURCE) ;
    AUTO__IO.CLOSE(DEST) ;
end COPY__AUTO__FILES ;
```

12.4 DIRECT FILE OPERATIONS

Text files and sequential files share an important limitation: we cannot access values in the middle of them without first reading all the values in front. In other words, we cannot move directly to a particular location in these files. If we want to process all the components of a file in the order of their locations, then sequential processing will be adequate. For those cases when we want to process components selectively, however, Ada provides *direct* files.

Each component of a direct file has an identifying number, called its *index*. An index value is an integer of type COUNT. The first component of a direct file has the index value 1. (You will recall that Ada also provides a subtype of COUNT named POSITIVE__COUNT.) The generic library package DIRECT__IO provides subprograms that allow us to reference file components by their indices.

The file management subprograms in DIRECT__IO are the same as those in SEQUENTIAL__IO. An additional file mode is available for direct files, however. Enumeration type FILE__MODE is expanded in DIRECT__IO to include INOUT__FILE. Unlike files of mode IN__FILE or OUT__FILE, a file of mode INOUT__FILE is available for both input and output.

For each direct file that is open, a *current index* is maintained. Procedure SET__INDEX allows us to move the current index to a new file position. Conversely, function INDEX returns the current index of the given file. Function SIZE returns the number of components in the file. Here are the specifications for these subprograms:

```
procedure SET__INDEX(FILE : FILE__TYPE;
                     TO : POSITIVE__COUNT);
function INDEX(FILE : FILE__TYPE) return POSITIVE__COUNT;
function SIZE(FILE : FILE__TYPE) return POSITIVE__COUNT;
```

Each call to READ or WRITE advances the current index of the file by one. Here is a statement sequence that reads the fifth component of a file, leaving the current index equal to 6:

```
SET__INDEX(MY__FILE,5);
READ(MY__FILE,TEMP);
```

To read a component and then update it in place, we must set the current index back before writing. Otherwise, the wrong component will be updated. Here is a statement sequence that reads the tenth component of a file of integers, increments the component, and then replaces it:

```
SET__INDEX(FILE => INT__FILE,TO => 10);
READ(INT__FILE, NUM);
NUM := NUM + 1;
SET__INDEX(INT__FILE,10);
WRITE(INT__FILE, NUM);
```

Additional forms of READ and WRITE are provided by DIRECT__IO so that calls to SET__INDEX are not always needed. These forms accept a third parameter, named TO, which specifies the desired index. Here is a statement sequence that duplicates the sequence above:

```
READ(INT__FILE, NUM,10);
NUM := NUM + 1;
WRITE(INT__FILE, NUM,10);
```

Here is a statement that reads the *last* component of INT__FILE:

```
READ(FILE => INT__FILE,ITEM => NUM,TO => SIZE(INT__FILE));
```

Example 12.7 shows a procedure that opens a direct file and searches for a specific component. The procedure accepts a dataset name and an integer number as parameters. It returns the index number corresponding to the component, if it is found, and the value 0 if not. The procedure assumes that the file components are in ascending order.

Example 12.7

```
with DIRECT__IO;
function FIND__ID(EXT__NAME : STRING; ID : INTEGER) return COUNT is
    --Employs a binary search to see whether ID is in the dataset.
    --EXT__NAME is the name of the dataset.
    --If ID is found, we return its component number.
    --If not, we return 0.
    NUM : INTEGER;
    LOWER,MID,UPPER : POSITIVE__COUNT;
    package INT__DIRECT is new DIRECT__IO(INTEGER);
    use INT__DIRECT;
    ID__FILE : FILE__TYPE;
begin
    OPEN(ID__FILE, EXT__NAME, IN__FILE);
    LOWER := 1;
    UPPER := SIZE(ID__FILE);
    while LOWER <= UPPER loop
        MID := (UPPER+LOWER)/2;
        READ(ID__FILE, NUM,MID);
        if NUM = ID then
            return MID;
        elsif NUM > ID then
            UPPER := MID-1;
        else
            LOWER := MID+1;
        end if;
    end loop;
    return 0;      --we didn't find it
end FIND__ID;
```

Appendix A

RESERVED WORDS

The list below gives Ada's reserved words. A declared identifier in an Ada program cannot conflict with a reserved word. The words marked with an asterisk in this list are associated with advanced language features that are not examined in this book.

```
abort *        exception     procedure
abs            exit          raise
accept *       for           range
access         function      record
all            generic       rem
and            goto          renames
array          if            return
at *           in            reverse
begin          is            select *
body           limited       separate *
case           loop          subtype
constant       mod           task *
declare *      new           terminate *
delay *        not           then
delta          null          type
digits         of            use
do             others        when
else           out           while
elsif          package       with
end            pragma        xor
entry *        private
```

Appendix B

ASCII CHARACTER SET

Character	Position Number
null (NUL)	0
ctrl/A (SOH)	1
ctrl/B (STX)	2
ctrl/C (ETX)	3
ctrl/D (EOT)	4
ctrl/E (ENQ)	5
ctrl/F (ACK)	6
ctrl/G (BEL)	7
ctrl/H (BS)	8
ctrl/I (HT)	9
ctrl/J (LF)	10
ctrl/K (VT)	11
ctrl/L (FF)	12
ctrl/M (CR)	13
ctrl/N (SO)	14
ctrl/O (SI)	15
ctrl/P (DLE)	16
ctrl/Q (DC1)	17
ctrl/R (DC2)	18
ctrl/S (DC3)	19
ctrl/T (DC4)	20
ctrl/U (NAK)	21
ctrl/V (SYN)	22
ctrl/W (ETB)	23
ctrl/X (CAN)	24
ctrl/Y (EM)	25
ctrl/Z (SUB)	26
escape (ESC)	27

Character	Position Number
(FS)	28
(GS)	29
(RS)	30
(US)	31
spacebar	32
!	33
″	34
#	35
$	36
%	37
&	38
’	39
(	40
)	41
*	42
+	43
,	44
−	45
.	46
/	47
0	48
1	49
2	50
. . .	
7	55
8	56
9	57
:	58
;	59
<	60
=	61
>	62
?	63
@	64
A	65
B	66
C	67
. . .	
X	88
Y	89
Z	90
[	91
\	92
]	93
∧	94
-	95
′	96
a	97
b	98
c	99
. . .	

<table>
<tr><th>Character</th><th>Position Number</th></tr>
<tr><td>x</td><td>120</td></tr>
<tr><td>y</td><td>121</td></tr>
<tr><td>z</td><td>122</td></tr>
<tr><td>{</td><td>123</td></tr>
<tr><td>|</td><td>124</td></tr>
<tr><td>}</td><td>125</td></tr>
<tr><td>~</td><td>126</td></tr>
<tr><td>delete (DEL)</td><td>127</td></tr>
</table>

Appendix C

LIBRARY PACKAGE STANDARD

```
package STANDARD is

    type BOOLEAN is (FALSE, TRUE);

    -- The predefined relational operators for this type are as follows:

    -- function "="  (LEFT, RIGHT : BOOLEAN) return BOOLEAN;
    -- function "/=" (LEFT, RIGHT : BOOLEAN) return BOOLEAN;
    -- function "<"  (LEFT, RIGHT : BOOLEAN) return BOOLEAN;
    -- function "<=" (LEFT, RIGHT : BOOLEAN) return BOOLEAN;
    -- function ">"  (LEFT, RIGHT : BOOLEAN) return BOOLEAN;
    -- function ">=" (LEFT, RIGHT : BOOLEAN) return BOOLEAN;

    -- The logical operators and the logical negation operator are explicitly
    -- declared:

    function "and"  (LEFT, RIGHT : BOOLEAN) return BOOLEAN;
    function "or"   (LEFT, RIGHT : BOOLEAN) return BOOLEAN;
    function "xor"  (LEFT, RIGHT : BOOLEAN) return BOOLEAN;

    function "not"  (RIGHT : BOOLEAN) return BOOLEAN;


    -- The universal type universal integer is predefined.

    type INTEGER is implementation defined;

    -- The predefined operators for this type are as follows:

    -- function "="  (LEFT, RIGHT : INTEGER) return BOOLEAN;
    -- function "/=" (LEFT, RIGHT : INTEGER) return BOOLEAN;
    -- function "<"  (LEFT, RIGHT : INTEGER) return BOOLEAN;
    -- function "<=" (LEFT, RIGHT : INTEGER) return BOOLEAN;
```

```
-- function ">"   (LEFT, RIGHT : INTEGER) return BOOLEAN;
-- function ">="  (LEFT, RIGHT : INTEGER) return BOOLEAN;
-- function "+"   (RIGHT : INTEGER) return INTEGER;
-- function "-"   (RIGHT : INTEGER) return INTEGER;
-- function "abs" (RIGHT : INTEGER) return INTEGER;

-- function "+"   (LEFT, RIGHT : INTEGER) return INTEGER;
-- function "-"   (LEFT, RIGHT : INTEGER) return INTEGER;
-- function "*"   (LEFT, RIGHT : INTEGER) return INTEGER;
-- function "/"   (LEFT, RIGHT : INTEGER) return INTEGER;
-- function "rem" (LEFT, RIGHT : INTEGER) return INTEGER;
-- function "mod" (LEFT, RIGHT : INTEGER) return INTEGER;

-- function "**"  (LEFT : INTEGER; RIGHT : INTEGER) return INTEGER;


-- The universal type universal real is predefined.


type FLOAT is implementation defined;

-- The predefined operators for this type are as follows:

-- function "="   (LEFT, RIGHT : FLOAT) return BOOLEAN;
-- function "/="  (LEFT, RIGHT : FLOAT) return BOOLEAN;
-- function "<"   (LEFT, RIGHT : FLOAT) return BOOLEAN;
-- function "<="  (LEFT, RIGHT : FLOAT) return BOOLEAN;
-- function ">"   (LEFT, RIGHT : FLOAT) return BOOLEAN;
-- function ">="  (LEFT, RIGHT : FLOAT) return BOOLEAN;

-- function "+"   (RIGHT : FLOAT) return FLOAT;
-- function "-"   (RIGHT : FLOAT) return FLOAT;
-- function "abs" (RIGHT : FLOAT) return FLOAT;

-- function "+"   (LEFT, RIGHT : FLOAT) return FLOAT;
-- function "-"   (LEFT, RIGHT : FLOAT) return FLOAT;
-- function "*"   (LEFT, RIGHT : FLOAT) return FLOAT;
-- function "/"   (LEFT, RIGHT : FLOAT) return FLOAT;

-- function "**"  (LEFT : FLOAT; RIGHT : INTEGER) return FLOAT;


-- In addition, the following operators are predefined for universal types:

-- function "*" (LEFT : universal integer;
                 RIGHT : universal real) return universal real;
-- function "*" (LEFT : universal real;
                 RIGHT : universal integer) return universal real;
-- function "/" (LEFT : universal real;
                 RIGHT : universal integer) return universal
-- The type universal fixed is predefined.
-- The only operators declared for this type are

-- function "*" (LEFT : any fixed point type;
                 RIGHT : any fixed point type) return universal fixed;
-- function "/" (LEFT : any fixed point type;
                 RIGHT : any fixed point type) return universal fixed;


-- The following characters form the standard ASCII character set.
-- Character literals corresponding to control characters are not
-- identifiers; they are indicated in italics in this definition.
```

```
type CHARACTER is

     (nul,   soh,   stx,   etx,      eot,   enq,   ack,   bel,
      bs,    ht,    lf,    vt,       ff,    cr,    so,    si,
      dle,   dc1,   dc2,   dc3,      dc4,   nak,   syn,   etb,
      can,   em,    sub,   esc,      fs,    gs,    rs,    us,

      ' ',   '!',   '"',   '#',      '$',   '%',   '&',   ''',
      '(',   ')',   '*',   '+',      ',',   '-',   '.',   '/',
      '0',   '1',   '2',   '3',      '4',   '5',   '6',   '7',
      '8',   '9',   ':',   ';',      '<',   '=',   '>',   '?',

      '@',   'A',   'B',   'C',      'D',   'E',   'F',   'G',
      'H',   'I',   'J',   'K',      'L',   'M',   'N',   'O',
      'P',   'Q',   'R',   'S',      'T',   'U',   'V',   'W',
      'X',   'Y',   'Z',   '[',      '\',   ']',   '^',   '_',
      '`',   'a',   'b',   'c',      'd',   'e',   'f',   'g',
      'h',   'i',   'j',   'k',      'l',   'm',   'n',   'o',
      'p',   'q',   'r',   's',      't',   'u',   'v',   'w',
      'x',   'y',   'z',   '{',      '|',   '}',   '~',   del);


-- The predefined operators for the type CHARACTER are the same as
-- for any enumeration type.


package ASCII is

   -- Control characters:

   NUL        : constant CHARACTER := nul;
   SOH        : constant CHARACTER := soh;
   STX        : constant CHARACTER := stx;
   ETX        : constant CHARACTER := etx;
   EOT        : constant CHARACTER := eot;
   ENQ        : constant CHARACTER := enq;
   ACK        : constant CHARACTER := ack;
   BEL        : constant CHARACTER := bel;
   BS         : constant CHARACTER := bs;
   HT         : constant CHARACTER := ht;
   LF         : constant CHARACTER := lf;
   VT         : constant CHARACTER := vt;
   FF         : constant CHARACTER := ff;
   CR         : constant CHARACTER := cr;
   SO         : constant CHARACTER := so;
   SI         : constant CHARACTER := si;
   DLE        : constant CHARACTER := dle;
   DC1        : constant CHARACTER := dc1;
   DC2        : constant CHARACTER := dc2;
   DC3        : constant CHARACTER := dc3;
   DC4        : constant CHARACTER := dc4;
   NAK        : constant CHARACTER := nak;
   SYN        : constant CHARACTER := syn;
   ETB        : constant CHARACTER := etb;
   CAN        : constant CHARACTER := can;
   EM         : constant CHARACTER := em;
   SUB        : constant CHARACTER := sub;
```

```
    ESC          : constant CHARACTER := esc;
    FS           : constant CHARACTER := fs;
    GS           : constant CHARACTER := gs;
    RS           : constant CHARACTER := rs;
    US           : constant CHARACTER := us;
    DEL          : constant CHARACTER := del;

    -- Other characters:

    EXCLAM       : constant CHARACTER := '!';
    QUOTATION    : constant CHARACTER := '"';
    SHARP        : constant CHARACTER := '#';
    DOLLAR       : constant CHARACTER := '$';
    PERCENT      : constant CHARACTER := '%';
    AMPERSAND    : constant CHARACTER := '&';
    COLON        : constant CHARACTER := ':';
    SEMICOLON    : constant CHARACTER := ';';
    QUERY        : constant CHARACTER := '?';
    AT_SIGN      : constant CHARACTER := '@';
    L_BRACKET    : constant CHARACTER := '[';
    BACK_SLASH   : constant CHARACTER := '\';
    R_BRACKET    : constant CHARACTER := ']';
    CIRCUMFLEX   : constant CHARACTER := '^';
    UNDERLINE    : constant CHARACTER := '_';
    GRAVE        : constant CHARACTER := '`';
    L_BRACE      : constant CHARACTER := '{';
    BAR          : constant CHARACTER := '|';
    R_BRACE      : constant CHARACTER := '}';
    TILDE        : constant CHARACTER := '~';

    -- Lowercase letters:

    LC_A : constant CHARACTER := 'a';
    ...
    LC_Z : constant CHARACTER := 'z';

end ASCII;


-- Predefined subtypes:

subtype NATURAL is INTEGER range 0..INTEGER'LAST;
subtype POSITIVE is INTEGER range 1..INTEGER'LAST;


-- Predefined string type:

type STRING is array(POSITIVE range <>) of CHARACTER;

pragma PACK(STRING);

-- The predefined operators for this type are as follows:

-- function "="   (LEFT, RIGHT : STRING) return BOOLEAN;
-- function "/"   (LEFT, RIGHT : STRING) return BOOLEAN;
-- function "<"   (LEFT, RIGHT : STRING) return BOOLEAN;
-- function "<="  (LEFT, RIGHT : STRING) return BOOLEAN;
-- function ">"   (LEFT, RIGHT : STRING) return BOOLEAN;
-- function ">="  (LEFT, RIGHT : STRING) return BOOLEAN;
```

```
-- function "&" (LEFT : STRING;     RIGHT : STRING)     return STRING;
-- function "&" (LEFT : CHARACTER;  RIGHT : STRING)     return STRING;
-- function "&" (LEFT : STRING;     RIGHT : CHARACTER)  return STRING;
-- function "&" (LEFT : CHARACTER;  RIGHT : CHARACTER)  return STRING;


type DURATION is delta implementation defined range implementation defined;

-- The predefined operators for the type
-- duration are the same as for any fixed-point type.

-- The predefined exceptions:

CONSTRAINT_ERROR : exception;
NUMERIC_ERROR    : exception;
PROGRAM_ERROR    : exception;
STORAGE_ERROR    : exception;
TASKING_ERROR    : exception;

end STANDARD;
```

Appendix D

LIBRARY PACKAGE TEXT_IO

```
with IO__EXCEPTIONS;
package TEXT__IO is

    type FILE__TYPE is limited private;

    type FILE__MODE is (IN__FILE, OUT__FILE);

    type COUNT is range 0 .. implementation defined;

    subtype POSITIVE__COUNT is COUNT range 1 .. COUNT'LAST;

    subtype FIELD          is INTEGER range 0 .. implementation defined;
    subtype NUMBER__BASE is INTEGER range 2 .. 16;

    UNBOUNDED : constant COUNT := 0; -- line and page length


    -- File Management

    procedure CREATE(FILE : in out FILE__TYPE;
                     MODE : in FILE__MODE := OUT__FILE;
                     NAME : in STRING      := " ";
                     FORM : in STRING      := " ");

    procedure OPEN(FILE : in out FILE__TYPE;
                   MODE : in FILE__MODE;
                   NAME : in STRING;
                   FORM : in STRING := " ");

    procedure CLOSE    (FILE : in out FILE__TYPE);
    procedure DELETE   (FILE : in out FILE__TYPE);
```

```
procedure RESET (FILE : in out FILE__TYPE; MODE : in FILE__MODE);
procedure RESET (FILE : in out FILE__TYPE);

function  MODE (FILE : in FILE__TYPE) return FILE__MODE;
function  NAME (FILE : in FILE__TYPE) return STRING;
function  FORM (FILE : in FILE__TYPE) return STRING;

function  IS__OPEN(FILE : in FILE__TYPE) return BOOLEAN;


-- Control of default input and output files

procedure SET__INPUT  (FILE : in FILE__TYPE);
procedure SET__OUTPUT(FILE : IN FILE__TYPE);

function STANDARD__INPUT  return FILE__TYPE;
function STANDARD__OUTPUT return FILE__TYPE;

function CURRENT__INPUT   return FILE__TYPE;
function CURRENT__OUTPUT  return FILE__TYPE;


-- Specification of line and page lengths

procedure SET__LINE__LENGTH(FILE : in FILE__TYPE; TO : in COUNT);
procedure SET__LINE__LENGTH(TO : in COUNT);

procedure SET__PAGE__LENGTH(FILE : in FILE__TYPE; TO : in COUNT);
procedure SET__PAGE__LENGTH(TO : in COUNT);

function  LINE__LENGTH(FILE : in FILE__TYPE) return COUNT;
function  LINE__LENGTH return COUNT;

function  PAGE__LENGTH(FILE : in FILE__TYPE) return COUNT;
function  PAGE__LENGTH return COUNT;


-- Column, Line, and Page Control

procedure NEW__LINE     (FILE : in FILE__TYPE;
                         SPACING : in POSITIVE__COUNT := 1);
procedure NEW__LINE     (SPACING : in POSITIVE__COUNT := 1);

procedure SKIP__LINE    (FILE : in FILE__TYPE;
                         SPACING : in POSITIVE__COUNT := 1);
procedure SKIP__LINE    (SPACING : in POSITIVE__COUNT := 1);

function  END__OF__LINE (FILE : in FILE__TYPE) return BOOLEAN;
function  END__OF__LINE  return BOOLEAN;

procedure NEW__PAGE     (FILE : in FILE__TYPE);
procedure NEW__PAGE;

procedure SKIP__PAGE    (FILE : in FILE__TYPE);
procedure SKIP__PAGE;

function  END__OF__PAGE(FILE : in FILE__TYPE) return BOOLEAN;
function  END__OF__PAGE return BOOLEAN;

function  END__OF__FILE (FILE : in FILE__TYPE) return BOOLEAN;
function  END__OF__FILE  return BOOLEAN;

procedure SET__COL  (FILE: in FILE__TYPE; TO : in POSITIVE__COUNT);
procedure SET__COL  (TO   : in POSITIVE__COUNT);
```

```
procedure SET__LINE(FILE: in FILE__TYPE; TO : in POSITIVE__COUNT);
procedure SET__LINE(TO   : in POSITIVE__COUNT);

function COL  (FILE : in FILE__TYPE) return POSITIVE__COUNT;
function COL   return POSITIVE__COUNT;

function LINE  (FILE : in FILE__TYPE) return POSITIVE__COUNT;
function LINE  return POSITIVE__COUNT;

function PAGE  (FILE : in FILE__TYPE) return POSITIVE__COUNT;
function PAGE  return POSITIVE__COUNT;


-- Character Input–Output

procedure GET(FILE  : in   FILE__TYPE; ITEM  : out CHARACTER);
procedure GET(ITEM : out  CHARACTER);
procedure PUT(FILE  : in   FILE__TYPE; ITEM  : in CHARACTER);
procedure PUT(ITEM : in   CHARACTER);


-- String Input–Output

procedure GET(FILE  : in  FILE__TYPE; ITEM  : out STRING);
procedure GET(ITEM : out STRING);
procedure PUT(FILE  : in  FILE__TYPE; ITEM  : in STRING);
procedure PUT(ITEM : in STRING);

procedure GET__LINE(FILE  : in FILE__TYPE; ITEM : out STRING;
                                LAST : out NATURAL);
procedure GET__LINE(ITEM : out STRING; LAST : out NATURAL);
procedure PUT__LINE(FILE  : in FILE__TYPE; ITEM : in STRING);
procedure PUT__LINE(ITEM : in STRING);


-- Generic package for Input–Output of Integer Types

generic
    type NUM is range <>;
package INTEGER__IO is

    DEFAULT__WIDTH : FIELD := NUM'WIDTH;
    DEFAULT__BASE   : NUMBER__BASE := 10;

    procedure GET(FILE   : in  FILE__TYPE; ITEM : out NUM;
                           WIDTH : in FIELD := 0);
    procedure GET(ITEM   : out NUM; WIDTH : in FIELD := 0);

    procedure PUT(FILE   : in  FILE__TYPE;
                  ITEM   : in  NUM;
                  WIDTH  : in  FIELD := DEFAULT__WIDTH;
                  BASE   : in  NUMBER__BASE := DEFAULT__BASE);
    procedure PUT(ITEM   : in  NUM;
                  WIDTH  : in  FIELD := DEFAULT__WIDTH;
                  BASE   : in  NUMBER__BASE := DEFAULT__BASE);

    procedure GET(FROM  : in  STRING; ITEM : out NUM;
                           LAST : out POSITIVE);
    procedure PUT(TO     : out STRING;
                  ITEM   : in  NUM;
                  BASE   : in  NUMBER__BASE := DEFAULT__BASE);

end INTEGER__IO;
```

```
-- Generic packages for Input–output of Real Types


generic
    type NUM is digits <>;
package FLOAT___IO is


    DEFAULT___FORE : FIELD := 2;
    DEFAULT___AFT  : FIELD := NUM'DIGITS - 1;
    DEFAULT___EXP  : FIELD := 3;
    procedure GET(FILE : in FILE___TYPE; ITEM : out NUM;
                             WIDTH : in FIELD := 0)
    procedure GET(ITEM : out NUM; WIDTH : in FIELD := 0);

    procedure PUT(FILE  : in  FILE___TYPE;
                  ITEM  : in  NUM;
                  FORE  : in  FIELD := DEFAULT___FORE;
                  AFT   : in  FIELD := DEFAULT___AFT;
                  EXP   : in  FIELD := DEFAULT___EXP);
    procedure PUT(ITEM  : in  NUM;
                  FORE  : in  FIELD := DEFAULT___FORE;
                  AFT   : in  FIELD := DEFAULT___AFT;
                  EXP   : in  FIELD := DEFAULT___EXP);

    procedure GET(FROM : in  STRING; ITEM : out NUM;
                             LAST : out POSITIVE);
    procedure PUT(TO    : out STRING;
                  ITEM  : in  NUM;
                  AFT   : in  FIELD := DEFAULT___AFT;
                  EXP   : in  FIELD := DEFAULT___EXP);

end FLOAT___IO;


generic
    type NUM is delta <>;
package FIXED___IO is

    DEFAULT___FORE : FIELD := NUM'FORE;
    DEFAULT___AFT  : FIELD := NUM'AFT;
    DEFAULT___EXP  : FIELD := 0;

    procedure GET(FILE  : in  FILE___TYPE; ITEM : out NUM;
                              WIDTH : in FIELD := 0);
    procedure GET(ITEM  : out NUM; WIDTH : in FIELD := 0);

    procedure PUT(FILE  : in  FILE___TYPE;
                  ITEM  : in  NUM;
                  FORE  : in  FIELD := DEFAULT___FORE;
                  AFT   : in  FIELD := DEFAULT___AFT;
                  EXP   : in  FIELD := DEFAULT___EXP);
    procedure PUT(ITEM  : in  NUM;
                  FORE  : in  FIELD := DEFAULT___FORE;
                  AFT   : in  FIELD := DEFAULT___AFT;
                  EXP   : in  FIELD := DEFAULT___EXP);

    procedure GET(FROM : in  STRING; ITEM : out NUM; LAST : out POSITIVE);
    procedure PUT(TO    : out STRING;
                  ITEM  : in  NUM;
```

```
               AFT        : in  FIELD := DEFAULT__AFT;
               EXP        : in  FIELD := DEFAULT__EXP);

end FIXED__IO;


-- Generic package for Input–Output of Enumeration Types

generic
    type ENUM is (<>);
package ENUMERATION__IO is

    DEFAULT__WIDTH : FIELD := 0;
    DEFAULT__IS__LC : BOOLEAN ;= FALSE; -- upper case

    procedure GET(FILE  : in  FILE__TYPE; ITEM : out ENUM);
    procedure GET(ITEM  : out ENUM);

    procedure PUT(FILE  : in  FILE__TYPE;
               ITEM     : in  ENUM;
               WIDTH    : in  FIELD    := DEFAULT__WIDTH;
               LC       : in  BOOLEAN := DEFAULT__IS__LC);
    procedure PUT(ITEM  : in  ENUM;
               WIDTH    : in  FIELD    := DEFAULT__WIDTH;
               LC       : in  BOOLEAN := DEFAULT__IS__LC);

    procedure GET(FROM : in  STRING; ITEM : out ENUM; LAST : out POSITIVE);
    procedure PUT(TO    : out STRING;
               ITEM     : in  ENUM;
               LC       : in  BOOLEAN := DEFAULT__IS__LC);
end ENUMERATION__IO;


-- Exceptions

STATUS__ERROR  : exception renames IO__EXCEPTIONS.STATUS__ERROR;
MODE__ERROR    : exception renames IO__EXCEPTIONS.MODE__ERROR;
NAME__ERROR    : exception renames IO__EXCEPTIONS.NAME__ERROR;
USE__ERROR     : exception renames IO__EXCEPTIONS.USE__ERROR;
DEVICE__ERROR  : exception renames IO__EXCEPTIONS.DEVICE__ERROR;
END__ERROR     : exception renames IO__EXCEPTIONS.END ERROR;
DATA__ERROR    : exception renames IO__EXCEPTIONS.DATA__ERROR;
LAYOUT__ERROR  : exception renames IO__EXCEPTIONS.LAYOUT__ERROR;


private
    -- implementation dependent
end TEXT__IO;
```

Index

abs operator, 4
Access constant, 84
Access variable, 82–84
AFT attribute, 43
Aggregate:
  and strings, 56
  array, 51–52
  record, 62
Allocation:
  composite type, 84–87
  scalar type, 82–84
and operator, 13–14, 46
Array:
  aggregate, 51–52
  assignment, 45, 53–54
  comparison, 45–46, 49
  component type, 44
  constrained, 44–48, 86
  dimensionality, 47
  index constraint, 49, 56
  index type, 44, 46
  slice, 52–54
  unconstrained, 48–50
ASCII character set, 55, 59, 135–37
Assignment, 2
Attribute inquiry, 34

BASE and formatting, 42–43
Based numbers, 41–42
Binary tree data structure, 90, 93–95
Body, 1
BOOLEAN type, 12–15, 29, 36

CALENDAR library package, 104–5
case, 18–20, 28–29, 36
Catenation operator, 58, 103
Character string, 10, 54
CHARACTER type, 54–55
Check, 108–9, 112
Closing file, 128–29
COL function, 124
Comment, 3–4
Comparison operator (*see* relational operator)
Composite type, 44
Constant declaration, 8–9
Control character, 59
Conversion function, 33, 38–39
COUNT type, 124
CREATE subprogram, 127
CURRENT_INPUT function, 128
CURRENT_OUTPUT function, 128

Dataset, 126
Declaration part, 1
Default file, 9
Deferred constant, 99–100
DELETE subprogram, 128
Delta, 39–40
DELTA attribute, 41
Derived type, 32–34, 80–81
Direct file, 131–33
DIRECT_IO package, 132
Discrete range, 31
Discrete type, 36

Elaboration, 9
END_OF_FILE function, 130
Enumeration type, 27–30
Exception, 108–14
Exceptional transfer, 25–26
exit, 20–23
EXP and formatting, 43
Exponentiation, 6, 40

File:
  closing, 126
  direct, 131–33
  external, 126
  mode, 126, 132
  opening, 126–27
  sequential, 129
  text, 124–29
FIRST attribute, 34, 41, 49, 50
Fixed point types, 39–41
FLOAT type, 39
Floating point types, 37–39
for loop, 23–25, 28, 31, 36
FORE attribute, 43
FORM function, 129
Formal object, 117

Formal subprogram, 121–23
Formal type, 116

Generic declaration, 115–23
GET subprogram, 4, 9, 57, 60, 124
GET_LINE subprogram, 60, 124, 127
goto statement, 25–26

Handler, 109–11
Header, 1

Identifier, 3, 134
if . . . then, 16–20
IMAGE attribute, 57
in operator, 14–15
INDEX function, 132
Instance, 115
Instantiation,
  and array types, 119–20
  and input-output, 9, 29, 34, 39, 40, 115, 130
  and private types, 119–20
  and scalar types, 115–18
INTEGER type, 2, 4–7, 36
IS_OPEN function, 129

Label, 25, 77
LAST attribute, 34, 41, 49, 50
LENGTH attribute, 50, 59
Library package, 103–5
Limited private type, 102–3
LINE_LENGTH function, 125
Linked list, 89, 90–93
Literal:
  boolean, 12
  character, 54–55
  enumeration, 27
  integer, 6–7, 41–42, 54
  real, 37, 42
Logical operator, 13–14
loop . . . exit, 20–21
Loop name, 23, 77
Loop parameter, 23–25, 31, 77

MACHINE_ROUNDS attribute, 41
Membership operator, 14–15
mod operator, 4–5, 38
Mode:
  of file, 126, 132
  of parameter, 74–75
MODE function, 129

NAME function, 129
NATURAL subtype, 31–32, 56, 60
Nested loop, 22–23
NEW_LINE subprogram, 10–11, 125
NEW_PAGE subprogram, 126
not operator, 13, 15
Null access value, 83
Null range, 25
Null statement, 19
Number declaration, 8–9
NUMBER_BASE subtype, 42

Object declaration, 7–9
OPEN subprogram, 127

Opening file, 126–27
or operator, 13–14, 46
Overloading, 29, 78–81, 117
Own variable, 99

Package, 96–107
PAGE function, 125
PAGE_LENGTH function, 125
POS attribute, 35–36, 55
Position number, 35–36, 55, 135
POSITIVE subtype, 31–32, 58
POSITIVE_COUNT type, 124
Pragma, 109
Precedence, 6, 15
PRED attribute, 35, 55
Private type, 99–103
Propagation, 110–11
PUT subprogram, 2, 9, 42–43, 57, 124
PUT_LINE subprogram, 11, 124

Qualification, 29, 78, 79

raise, 111–12
RANGE attribute, 50
Range constraint, 30–31, 38
READ subprogram, 129–30, 132
Record:
  aggregate, 62
  comparison, 62
  constant, 69
  constrained, 66
  discriminant, 64–65
  invariant, 61–64
  variant, 64–69, 100
Relational operator, 12–13, 28, 100, 103
rem operator, 5, 38
Renaming declaration, 64, 78, 98
Reserved word, 2, 3, 134
RESET subprogram, 128
return, 72, 74
Robustness, 113

Scalar types, 37
Scientific notation, 7
Scope rules, 76–78
Semicolons, 4
Sequential file, 129
SEQUENTIAL_IO library package, 129
SET_COL subprogram, 125–26
SET_INDEX subprogram, 132
SET_INPUT subprogram, 128
SET_LINE_LENGTH subprogram, 125
SET_OUTPUT subprogram, 128
SET_PAGE_LENGTH subprogram, 125
Short circuit control form, 14
Side effect, 102–3, 106
SIZE function, 132
Stack data structure, 87–90, 102–3, 112
STANDARD library package, 103, 138–42
String comparison, 56–57
STRING type, 56
String variables, 54–60
Subprogram:
  declarative part, 72
  function, 70–73

Subprogram (cont.):
  local identifiers, 72
  parameter, 71, 75
  parameter mode, 74–75
  procedure, 73–76
  recursive, 72–73
  specification, 71
Subtypes, 30–32
SUCC attribute, 35, 55
SUPPRESS pragma, 109

Text file, 124–29
TEXT_IO library package, 103, 124, 143–47
Traversal, binary tree, 95

Undefined value error, 7
use clause, 98

VAL attribute, 35–36, 55
VALUE attribute, 57
Visibility rules, 77–78, 97–98

while loop, 21–23
WIDTH and formatting, 42–43
with clause, 103
WRITE subprogram, 129–30, 132

xor operator, 13–14, 46